MODERN
QUILT
BIBLE

Over 100 techniques and design ideas
for the modern quilter

Elizabeth Betts

DAVID & CHARLES

CONTENTS

Welcome

Over the past fifteen years, modern quilting, as a term we know today, has grown in popularity and recognition to become a standout aesthetic in the international quilt community. This is due to many reasons, including how our lifestyles have affected the type of quilts we make, the way trends in quilting have developed faster due to the influence of the internet, and the role of professional groups – most importantly the Modern Quilt Guild – which have helped to define and promote modern quilting.

The actual aesthetic of a modern quilt is subjective so can vary slightly depending on who is defining it. However, widely accepted definitions include reference to design elements such as high colour contrast, negative space, asymmetry, alternative grid layout, and the updating of traditional designs in a new and often unexpected way. Design is at the core of categorising a modern quilt and it is this that I have been keen to explore in this book.

The Modern Quilt Bible is a book of two halves. The first half focuses on ten design concepts and ideas for modern quilting, and each design focus chapter includes a project for you to make. The second half features techniques that are commonly used to make modern quilts and, with step-by-step illustrations throughout, it aims to be your essential reference guide. I hope you enjoy using this book as part of your own unique modern quilt journey.

Liz

TOOLS AND EQUIPMENT

When it comes to the equipment required for making a quilt, you may have your own preferences, but this chapter aims to provide you with an overview. Some items are essential, while others are handy to have to make the process quicker or more accurate. New products are launched every month, so visit your local quilt shop often or look online.

For further information about relevant equipment, refer to the Machine Sewing, Hand Sewing Basics and Quilting chapters in the Quilt Basics section.

Iron

A regular domestic iron is ideal, but if investing in a new model an auto shut-off function, where the iron turns itself off then heats up again when used, is useful. Keep your iron clean and don't forget to change the temperature to the correct setting for your fabric.

Mini Iron

A small iron is useful when working on a quilt with lots of small patch piecing or appliqué. They are portable but if you can, keep yours to hand on a table next to your sewing machine to speed up the stitching and pressing process.

Ironing Board

Any domestic ironing board is adequate for quilt making: keep it clean and change the cover if it gets marked. If you make large quilts regularly, a bigger ironing board is handy as you can press more of the quilt at a time (some quilters convert a table to give as large a pressing area as possible). If you are often working on smaller patches, a small table-top ironing board is ideal; these generally include a board that sits on a table top, a mat that can be folded and put in a bag when not in use, and a cutting mat that has a pressing mat on one side.

Pressing Mat

Wool pressing mats can be a luxury addition to your kit. They are thick, and act as a resist when you press so you get a very flat seam. They also adhere to the fabric, which helps to prevent any distortion.

Seam Roller

For some projects, such as foundation piecing, a seam roller can be used for pressing seams. It has a wheel that you run along the seam to hold it in place. This works best with fabrics that can be easily creased such as 100% cotton.

Starch and Pressing Spray

A spray of starch can make fabric crisper, which can make it easier to cut and sew. For fabric that has wrinkles and creases, a pressing spray is helpful, such as Mary Ellen's Best Press.

Hand Sewing Needles

There are lots of different types and sizes available, but the most important thing to remember is to use the one most suited to what you are sewing. When not in use, store your needles in a needlebook or in the packet. For more information, refer to Quilt Basics: Sewing Basics.

Needle Threader

This inexpensive gizmo makes it easy to thread a hand sewing needle. Place the fine wire loop through the eye of the needle, place the thread through the loop, then pull the loop back through the eye. (They can also be used to thread a sewing machine needle.) If you often use a needle threader when hand sewing, it may be worth investing in an automatic needle threader.

Thimble

A thimble protects your fingers when hand sewing or quilting and helps to push the needle through the fabric. The traditional dome style comes in metal or plastic versions and different sizes so you can find one that feels comfortable. There are also leather and adhesive thimbles which some quilters find easier to use and are often used on the bottom finger when hand quilting in a frame. If you don't usually use a thimble test a few before purchasing to find what type suits you.

Sewing Machine

Although you can get machines with a host of different functions to make machine quilting quicker and easier, any sewing machine that sews a straight stitch can be used for making quilts. If you look after it well, your sewing machine will serve you for many years. For more information, refer to Quilt Basics: Sewing Basics.

Machine Sewing Needles

There are different types available, depending on what you are sewing. For more information, refer to Quilt Basics: Sewing Basics.

Pins

Pins should glide through the fabric easily without damaging the material. Try to use a fine pin so the hole it makes in the fabric is small. Long pins are good for piecing while small pins are best for appliqué or piecing with small units as they are less likely to catch on the sewing thread. Always discard pins that are blunt or bent as they may make a hole in your fabric. Keep a pin cushion close to hand when sewing.

Quilter's Safety Pins

These are used to hold the layers of a quilt together prior to sewing and they come in different sizes suitable for use with different waddings (battings), for example, you may want to use smaller ones for a thinner wadding and larger ones for a high loft wadding. Store them in a tin or jar and discard any that are blunt.

Binding Clips

These are handy for holding binding in place ready for sewing, and they are particularly useful when machine sewing binding to both sides of the quilt.

Scissors

If you are using scissors to cut fabric it is well worth investing in a good pair of dressmaking shears, and if you look after them, they should last a long time. Put them back in their sheath when not in use, get them sharpened regularly, and keep them clean. As well as achieving a clean and accurate cut, a good pair of shears will put less pressure on your hands. Use a strong pair of household scissors for cutting wadding (batting) to avoid blunting your shears. Also useful are small snips or embroidery scissors for trimming threads or for use with appliqué, and a pair of craft scissors for cutting paper and template plastic.

Stitch Unpick

Also known as a seam ripper, these come in different sizes and are indispensable for the mishaps that can happen while sewing. When not in use keep the cover on top of the sharp point; replace it if it starts to blunt.

Rotary Cutter

This is a handheld tool with a circular blade that makes cutting fabric easy, quick and accurate. There are a variety of sizes including 18mm and 28mm (suitable for cutting curves), 45mm (for regular cutting), and 60mm (for cutting lots of large pieces such as strips). It is important to work safely when using a rotary cutter (refer to Piecing: Patchwork Basics), on a suitable cutting surface, such as a self-healing mat. Always cover the blade when not in use.

Self-Healing Mat

These mats are designed for the blade of the rotary cutter to sink into, so a good mat will extend the life of your blade and make accurate cuts. They come in a variety of sizes, so you can choose one to suit your work surface, and have a grid marked on top which can help you keep your fabric straight.

Quilter's Rulers

These are made from thick, transparent acrylic, so they are easy to see through while being sufficiently sturdy for repetitive use. They form a barrier for the blade of the rotary cutter to follow and are available with lots of different types of markings that act as guidelines as you cut. These guidelines can be black, red or yellow lines so choose the ones that you find easiest to read. Quilter's rulers come in hundreds of different shapes and sizes, from small squares to hexagons and circles. When starting a long ruler, small square and large square are probably most useful, then buy others as needed; for example, if making a quilt that requires 200 equilateral triangles, you may want to invest in one specially designed for this purpose. Rulers are available in both imperial and metric but don't mix the two on the same project.

Tape Measure

A standard flexible tape with both imperial and metric markings is essential and if you make large quilts, look out for extra-long tape measures that enable you to measure a quilt in one go.

Yardstick

These long rulers are available in wood, plastic or metal and are useful for marking quilting lines across a quilt top. If you like to supersize blocks they can also be handy, for measuring and marking lines, for example when making half-square triangles.

Marking Tools

In quilt making there are various stages where the fabric may need to be marked, such as when sewing inset seams or quilting a specific design, and the tools used can include pencils, pens, chalk, pressure markers and tape. When using a marking tool, it is most important to test it first on a scrap of fabric to make sure the marks can be removed easily. For more information, refer to Quilt Basics: Sewing Basics and Quilting.

Fabric Glue

Look out for glue specially made for use on fabric that washes out, which is handy for preparing and temporarily positioning appliqué pieces. A fabric glue stick can also be used to hold fabric around paper templates when English paper piecing.

Basting Spray

This is a spray glue that can be used to hold the quilt top, wadding (batting) and backing together when layering a quilt.

Template Plastic or Card

These are used for making templates for piecing or quilting. For more information, refer to Quilt Basics: Sewing Basics and Quilting.

Freezer Paper

A versatile addition to a sewing kit, this paper is usually sold on a roll. It has a shiny (adhesive) side and a matt (paper) side and when the shiny side is placed on fabric and pressed it holds in place. After use, it peels off easily and leaves no residue. Uses can include making templates for English paper piecing and appliqué, marking quilting designs and creating stencils for fabric printing.

Threads

Generally it is recommended that you match the fibre of the thread to that of the fabric you are making your quilt from, so for cotton fabric use cotton thread; this means the thread should behave in the same way as the fabric and will age at the same rate, important if making an heirloom quilt. Sometimes you may choose a thread for its special characteristics, such as a fine silk for turned edge appliqué or shiny rayon for decorative machine quilting. Thread is graded by size and the smaller the number the thicker the thread (see Thread Weight box for more information). When machine stitching, the best results are gained from matching the weight of the top (needle) thread to the bottom (bobbin) thread, although you can experiment with this to create different effects. Look after your threads, keep them out of direct sunlight and in a box so they don't attract dust and are less likely to get tangled.

THREAD TERMS

When looking for threads you may come across the following terms:

Long staple cotton This type of cotton plant has longer fibres and therefore makes a stronger thread.

Mercerised Thread put through this process is stronger and develops a sheen.

Twisted This process makes a strong thread.

Invisible Usually made from nylon, this is a clear thread. It is mainly used for invisible machine appliqué and for quilting when you only want the texture, not the stitches, to be seen, or to be completely invisible if quilting in the ditch.

Metallic These are shiny threads suitable for quilting or for embroidery. It will often be necessary to use a special needle and for the tension to be altered on the sewing machine to prevent the thread from breaking, so test before use.

Variegated colour The thread has been dyed so that it changes colour, either graduating between different colours, or from light to dark of the same shade. As it is designed to be seen, it is ideal for quilting or decorative use. Variegated thread is available in lots of different weights.

Thread Weight	When to Use
60 weight and above	Super-fine threads suitable for sewing fine fabrics, and invisible hand appliqué and piecing. Also good for quilting where you want the stitching to create a texture rather than the quilting stitches to be seen. If free-motion quilting densely in areas, using a finer thread can help prevent the fabric becoming stiff, but do test first as thinner threads, by their nature, can sometimes be weaker, and so more likely to break.
50 weight	Fine enough to not affect seams (the finer the thread the flatter the finished seam), yet strong enough to hold a project together, this is the most common thread weight for piecing patchwork. Sometimes used for hand and machine quilting if a finer thread is required.
30 and 40 weight	Ideal for machine and hand quilting, or for piecing thick fabrics such as denim. The extra thickness makes the thread stronger and when quilting the stitches sit on top of the fabric adding more texture to the quilt.
8 and 12 weight	These thicker threads are best suited to decorative hand sewing and quilting; however, with a few tweaks, such as using a larger needle and a size 50 weight thread in the bobbin, or having the heavier weight thread in the bobbin and quilting with the wrong side up, they can be used in machine quilting.

TECHNOLOGY

In today's world, with the pace of innovation seeming to get faster each year, there is much potential to incorporate technology into quilt making. This can be as simple as using a digital camera, or may involve making the financial investment in a computerised sewing machine. It is good to be aware of the opportunities for enhancing your quilt making, such as designing using software or cutting fabric using a die cutter, so consider the options to see if they are right for you.

Is It Right for You?

The focus here is on how technology is being used to design and make quilts but there are often new products and services being launched so this area of quilt making is always evolving. This section is not designed to make clear recommendations but rather to open your eyes to the possibilities. Be in tune with your personal preferences, and remember that what one person loves another may dislike, so if you are interested in something but have never used it before, then try it out before you buy. Ask around friends and your quilt group, or if applicable see if the company will be demonstrating at a show. With most technology there is an initial financial cost and sometimes additional payments along the way, so it can be a good idea to check you are happy with it first. Also, if the purchase is for something portable, such as a cutting machine, you could share it with a friend or quilt group. If buying equipment, look out for second-hand deals online – you can always upgrade later but it means you can work out if and how much you will use something before making a major investment.

Photography

The evolution of digital and mobile phone photography has had immense benefits for quilters. It has a huge role to play across the whole process of quilt making, from recording ideas and inspiration to sharing the finished result. Photographs can also be used directly for design: take a snapshot of an interesting building, for example – the lines can be traced and then turned into a quilt block; and if you lack the confidence to draw a template for appliqué, just pick your subject, photograph it, and trace it off. And if you see an interesting colour combination when out and about, you can take a photo to store the idea for later.

When making a quilt, cameras are invaluable for being able to see how different layouts look. It is interesting how the camera can pick out things your eye does not, so if you are working with lots of different colours, it can give you a very different viewpoint of the layout. Also, at the press of a button, you can change the image into greyscale, which will pick out tones, so that you can see how these are distributed across the piece of work.

Another important role for a well-timed digital photo is to help you to keep track of fabric placement. When it has taken a long time to decide on where fabrics will be positioned in a quilt, but others need to be able to cross the dining room floor to get to their dinner, a quick click and everything can be packed away, leaving you confident that when you have time to sew again you'll know exactly what goes where.

Professional Design Software

There are many products on the market that can be used for design, not specifically for quilts, but useful to those designing quilts nevertheless. Some use a desktop computer only, whilst others have the additional advantage of being used via an app. The most popular ones are Photoshop, Illustrator and Corel Draw. Corel Draw, the predecessor to the other two, is a vector-based design software that can also be used for photo editing, mainly on PCs. Although Photoshop is mainly professionally used for photo editing and retouching, it has a whole host of other options too, such as drawing wavy lines, tracing and colouring in blocks of colour, so you can almost see what your finished quilt will look like. Illustrator, as its name suggests, is a vector program designed specifically for drawing and tracing, and designs can be scaled up to very large sizes, which makes it very popular for making templates and patterns. Anecdotally, Photoshop has a reputation for being easier to learn than Illustrator, but this will very much depend on the individual and their previous experience.

For instruction, there are books, online videos, as well as tutorials and workshops run by education centres. However, using this software can be costly, so look out for free trials before making an investment, or ask a friend who already uses one of these programs to show you how they work. Before purchasing, make sure you buy the right PC or Mac compatible version, and as you can end up with very large file sizes, check your computer has sufficient memory to run the software. A good starting point can be to use the program to design a quilt you have already made as a template, as this means that you will focus on the process and not be distracted by functions such as changing colours and tweaking designs. It can be easy to get side tracked though as the functions are so vast, and you may find that your problem is not coming up with the ideas but finding the time to make them.

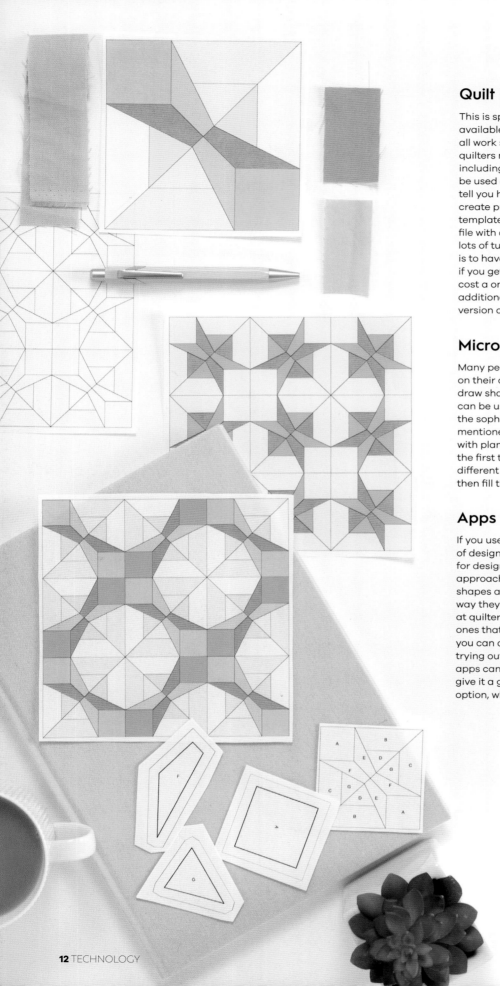

Quilt Design Software

This is specifically designed for quilters and products available include Electric Quilt and Quilt Pro. They all work slightly differently but being designed for quilters means they have lots of specific functions, including block designs and fabric prints, that can be used at the press of a button. They can also tell you how much fabric you need for a quilt and create printable templates. The foundation piecing templates can be very useful producing a printable file with a fine and accurate line. The products have lots of tutorials online, although the best way to learn is to have a go at designing what you want, then if you get stuck look online for help. They usually cost a one-off fee, although there is sometimes an additional charge if you want to upgrade your old version of the software to a newer one.

Microsoft Word and Paint

Many people have these two software programs on their computers without realising that they can draw shapes using them and that, therefore, they can be used for quilt design. While they do not have the sophistication of the software programs already mentioned, they are easy to use and can be helpful with planning a quilt. If designing on one of them for the first time, have a go at drawing some shapes at different sizes and converting them to a single outline, then fill them in with colour.

Apps for Tablets

If you use a tablet or an iPad there are a whole range of design apps that can be downloaded and used for designing quilts. They are for general design, so approach them in the same way as Word, drawing shapes and changing colours to get to grips with the way they work. There are also apps aimed specifically at quilters and, if you like making pixellated quilts, ones that will turn an image into squares. Apps where you can draw on top of photos can be really good for trying out different quilting designs. The price of the apps can vary, but most offer free versions so you can give it a go before upgrading to the more expensive option, which unlocks more features.

Cutting Machines

Die cutting is where fabric (or another material such as paper) is placed on a die and put through a machine to cut the fabric. The die has a blade the same size as the shape to be cut, then for safety a protective layer on top. When the die goes through the machine, pressure is placed on the die, which pushes the material into the blade and so the material is cut, and you get exactly the same shape each time. They can make cutting shapes such as circles fast and accurate. There are limitations in that you are dependent on the manufacturer having the right shape and size of die to suit your project, and buying the machine and die is an initial investment. However, they do speed up the sewing process, particularly if making a quilt with curved pieces, such as quarter circle units.

Digital cutting machines have a blade inside them and the material is fed through and cuts according to where a computer file tells it to. This means it gives you lots of options for creating your own patches, lettering or appliqué motifs. They also cut paper, which is handy for preparing English paper piecing templates. The software needs a little bit of experience to work it, but there are many videos online and manufacturers support customer learning with information and demonstrations.

Computerised Sewing Machines

Many sewing machines now are computerised. Functions such as stitch width and length can be changed at the press of a button rather than by moving a dial, with additional features to manual sewing machines, such as the needle up/down facility which makes sure the needle always finishes where you want it. Higher end computerised machines offer additional decorative stitches, such as blanket stitch (handy for finishing appliqué), as well as text fonts (useful for personalising items or stitching quilt labels).

Embroidery machines sew a pre-programmed pattern, so you prepare the machine, place the fabric in a hoop, then press a button and it is stitched for you. They have pre-set designs or you can buy a specific design online, download it, then add that to your machine's library. You can also get additional software to enable you to design your own motifs. Embroidery machines can be great for making quilt labels and for adding stitch embellishment to a project, for example from a sketch. They can also be used for quilting, although will only stitch an area as big as the hoop, so for a big project it would need a lot of input to keep re-hooping the fabric.

Long-Arm Machines

These are large sewing machines designed specifically for quilting. They range from smaller versions where the operator can sit down (similar to operating a domestic sewing machine, but with a much larger throat space and used with the end facing the stitcher), to larger machines that can include a computer which controls the quilting design once the quilt top and backing has been loaded on the frame. They are quite an investment and need space, so most quilters either give their quilt top to a long-arm quilter to complete or hire the machine on-site at a quilt store, if they are lucky enough to have this service offered locally. Prices vary depending on location, the time it will take and the type of quilting required. Ask for a quote in advance: most long-arm quilters will be able to give you options so you can keep within a budget, as well as getting the level of quilting that is specific to you and your quilt. Quilting designs range from allover patterns to custom intricate ruler work. Some companies can also digitise a quilt pattern to your own design. It may be useful to look up on the internet what long-arm services are available near you, or ask for recommendations from quilt shops or quilt groups.

FABRIC

In theory, any fabric can be used for modern quilt making, however some types of cloth are easier to sew than others and are more likely to give the desired finished look. If you get to know your fabrics then it makes it easier to choose the right one for your project.

Popular Quilting Fabrics

There are certain fabrics that are particularly popular among quilters due to their qualities such as how easy they are to press and how they wash.

COTTON

Woven 100% cotton fabric is suited to making quilts as it is crisp and easy to press, but also has a drape. There are many different types of cotton available with some more appropriate for use in patchwork, such as craft-weight cotton (also known as quilter's cotton) for sale in quilt stores everywhere. Cotton lawn is a lightweight cotton that is commonly used and, although the smooth finish can mean it may require more pinning when sewing, it has a lovely soft feel to it. Double gauze and voile are two types of lightweight cotton fabric that are sometimes used in modern quilt making. Double gauze is made from two light layers of gauze held together at various points, while voile is a lightweight, almost sheer fabric. Both can be used with just a piece of fabric on the back to make a coverlet, or if not too sheer, with a thin wadding (batting) in between to make a quilt suitable for warm weather.

Heavyweight cotton fabrics can be used in quilt making, too, including furnishing weight, canvas cotton and denim. Whilst the bulkiness of the seams means these fabrics are unsuitable for small intricate projects, they can be useful for making hardwearing items such as bags and cushions, or for backing wall quilts, as the fabric thickness helps the project to keep its shape.

If you are sewing with new fabric or a different machine, test the stitching on some scrap fabric first before starting.

LINEN

As with cotton, this natural fabric comes in different weights and weaves. It tends to have a rougher finish than most cottons, so the texture of the cloth can add interest to a quilt. Some linens can have a fairly loose weave which can make it trickier to work with as the fabric can be difficult to cut straight and is more likely to fray. To counteract this, you can use a wider seam allowance than the standard ¼in and spray it with starch.

COTTON/LINEN BLENDS

These have a linen look and feel but the weight of the fabric is suited to quilt making as it can be handled in the same way as craft-weight (quilter's) cotton, so the two types can be mixed together. It has a matt finish and slightly textured surface and is popular in modern quilts.

Fabrics and Sustainability

In theory, any fabric can be used to make a quilt and the craft has a history of using what is available at that time – the Victorians were fans of silk and velvet, and in the 1960s and 1970s, polyester and polyester mix fabrics were widely used. With current environmental and socio-economic concerns, 'green' fabric is becoming increasingly important and this can include sourcing organic cotton, or dyeing your own fabric using vegetable dyes, or incorporating worn clothing into your quilts. For example, a selection of old shirts can make an interesting low-volume background: to prepare clothing for use, cut along the seams and open it out to make flat pieces of fabric, then cut and sew as usual.

▶ *Selection of fabrics including craft-weight cotton, cotton lawn, linen blend and denim repurposed from a dress.*

Fabric Preparation

To get the most out of your fabrics they need a little preparation before you start to cut and sew.

COMBINING DIFFERENT FABRIC WEIGHTS

Generally in quilt making, the best results tend to be achieved by using fabrics of a similar weight as the quilt will hang or drape evenly and the fabrics will react to being quilted and washed in the same way. However, when making a modern quilt you may want to mix different fabrics and textures: to counteract any issues, try to use the different fabrics evenly across the quilt, and if you think the weights may affect a quilt, do a test block before starting. You can also put fusible interfacing on the back of some fabrics before starting to make the weights more even.

PRE-WASHING FABRICS

The two main reasons to pre-wash are to prevent shrinkage and stop any dye running. If you are using a fabric with a loose weave that may fray, machine sew a wide zigzag around the edge before washing. Pre-cuts are usually not pre-washed, and if the project you are making will never be washed, such as a wall hanging, then you may want to skip this step.

PRESSING

Pressing your fabric well before sewing makes it more accurate to cut and sew. Use the right setting for the type of fabric and if needed test on a scrap first. Although steam is not recommended when piecing, it can be handy to remove creases from a fabric. Fabrics such as linen can be pressed just before they are completely dry from their pre-wash. You might want to use a pressing cloth, which is a piece of unbleached lightweight cotton or calico that is placed on top of the fabric before it is pressed. With fabrics that can go shiny when pressed, such as some linens, a pressing cloth will prevent this, and it also keeps your fabric clean in case your iron has residue on it from something such as fusible interfacing. If you are struggling to remove a crease, damp the cloth before pressing.

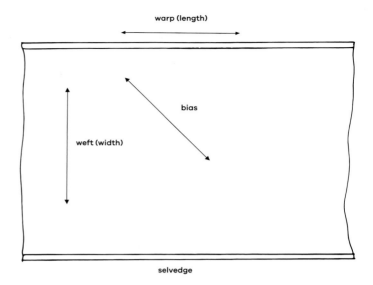

WORKING WITH WOVEN FABRIC

Woven cloth is made on a loom with the warp threads running along the length of the loom and the weft along the width. The 45-degree diagonal across a piece of fabric is the bias.

Warp, weft and bias influence how fabric behaves. The warp (length) does not stretch as much as the weft (width) so is less likely to distort when sewing. The bias has the most stretch so you should avoid cutting on the bias unless this is impossible (in the case of triangles), although sometimes this may be exactly what is required (in the case of making binding to go around a curved edge). When making quilts, cut fabric along the straight grain (parallel to the weft or warp) as this will give you a flatter and more precise finish as the fabric will not distort. The selvedge runs along the length of the fabric and these should be trimmed to get rid of the unsightly little holes that show where it was placed on the loom. Also, the selvedge can pull the fabric in, so cutting it off allows the threads to relax and allows for more accurate cutting.

How to Buy Fabric

When buying fabric from quilt shops there are different options for buying quantities. Which one you choose will depend on your project, but if you are buying fabric 'just in case' to add to your stash then look at the types of quilts you make. If they are large then you may want to purchase a yard at a time, if smaller quilts then a fat quarter is ideal.

OFF THE BOLT/ROLL

If plenty of fabric is in stock you can buy whatever quantity you want. Do check if the shop does a minimum amount, as it may be that you only need ¼yd but have to buy ½yd as this is the minimum amount they will sell. If a quilt pattern does not state the width of the fabric it will usually be based on craft-weight (quilter's) cotton from a standard 42in wide bolt (usable amount taking into account selvedges). Fabrics can come in different widths, although craft-weight cotton is usually 44 / 45in wide. This includes selvedge, so most designers base their fabric quantities for patterns based on fabric that is 42in wide.

FAT QUARTER

This is a ½yd cut from the bolt that has then been cut in half width ways (across the middle of the fabric). Each piece ends up with the selvedge on one side. An imperial fat quarter (cut from a ½yd) measures 18 x 22in. For some projects, fat quarters are more economical than buying a ¼yd of fabric cut from the bolt: for example, you can cut nine 6in squares from a fat quarter, but only seven from a ¼yd.

FAT EIGHTH

This is a fat quarter cut in half so an imperial fat eighth measures 9 x 22in. They are ideal for projects where you only need a small piece of fabric. For an even smaller piece, look out for fat sixteenths, that are half the size of a fat eighth.

PRE-CUTS

Pre-cuts are the name given to packs of fabric in a particular size, such as 5in squares or 2½in wide strips. They can be prepared by a manufacturer or by quilt shops, and they can use a whole collection from a designer, or are selected to go together. As well as speeding up the process when choosing fabric, they mean you can skip much of the cutting stage, or all of it if you are sewing them straight from the pack.

PATTERNS

Most fabric shops and websites also sell quilt patterns. Often beautifully packaged, they contain instructions and templates and are sometimes kitted up with fabric and threads. Even if you enjoy designing and planning your own quilts, there may be times when someone else's pattern tempts you. If following a bought pattern (or one from a book), first read though all the instructions. It can be tempting to only read the steps as you go but it is important to get the whole picture, for example, it may be more suitable for one fabric than another. Double check the measurements, to see if they recommend a scant ¼in, for example, or if you need to add seam allowance onto templates.

When you follow a pattern, think about how you can add your own take to it. This may be a little play with colour, or it could be deciding to make just one block up as a cushion. Finally, share a photo of your finished project on social media as an inspiration to others; tag the designer or look for a hashtag unique to the design to make it easy for others to find.

DESIGN
FOCUS

COLOUR

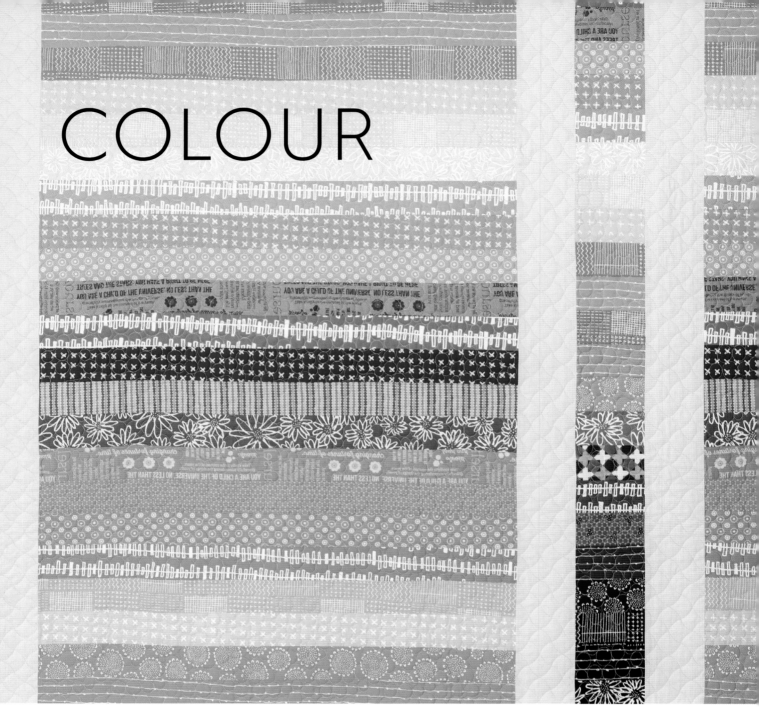

PHOTO CREDIT: Jason Jenkir

The power of colour is so strong it can be the one thing that makes someone attracted to a quilt design. When thinking about colour, there are lots of theories and strands to pull together and these are explored in this chapter. Do also be aware of your emotional response to colour: for example, you may love red, which is perceived as bright and attention seeking, or perhaps you are more of a green person, which, with its links to nature, is calming and peaceful. Quilters often find they are drawn to certain colours – a quick glance at a fabric stash usually reflects this.

▲ *Detail from the Boardwalk quilt (Pam and Nicky Lintott, **Jelly Roll Quilts in a Weekend**) is a vibrant example of what can be achieved by using colours on just one side of the colour wheel. The yellows, greens and blues relate to one another and have a powerful effect in the way they graduate from light to dark. The choice of fabric for the background gives the colours room to shine.*

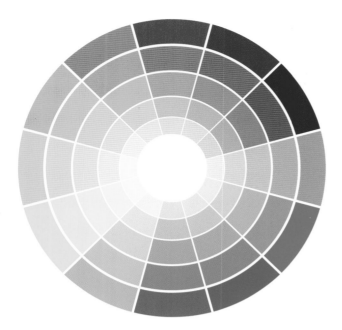

THE COLOUR WHEEL

The colour wheel is a tool that makes it easy to link colours together and explore how they relate to one another. Gaining an understanding of the colour wheel can help you when selecting fabrics for a quilt and increase your confidence in using colour, but don't ignore your instincts: if you like a particular colour combination and it works for you, have confidence in your choice. Modern quilts often feature an unexpected play with colour – for example, a quilt of regular identical blocks that features a single block where the colours have been reversed – so do experiment with ideas.

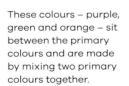

Primary colours

PRIMARY COLOURS

The wheel starts with the three primary colours of red, blue and yellow. From these, all other colours are formed.

Secondary colours

SECONDARY COLOURS

These colours – purple, green and orange – sit between the primary colours and are made by mixing two primary colours together.

Tertiary colours

TERTIARY COLOURS

These sit between the secondary colours and include red-orange, blue-purple and yellow-green.

EXPLORING COLOUR OPTIONS

The colour wheel can be used to explore many different colour options when selecting fabrics for a quilt.

Complementary colours

COMPLEMENTARY

This uses colours that are opposite to each other. Creating a strong contrast, it can make for a vivid looking quilt.

Analogous colours

ANALOGOUS

This uses three adjacent colours, for example red, red-violet and violet. It can be easy to work with and creates a calm, coordinated look in a quilt.

Split complementary colours

SPLIT COMPLEMENTARY

This combines one colour with the two that sit to either side of its complementary; it can be used to add small pops of unexpected colour in a quilt.

Rectangular tetradic complementary colours

RECTANGULAR TETRADIC COMPLEMENTARY

This uses two colours, separated by another colour, in combination with their complementary colours. It can create an exciting, bold effect.

Square tetradic complementary colours

SQUARE TETRADIC COMPLEMENTARY

This is a combination of four colours evenly spaced across the wheel. It can create an intense, dynamic look when used in a quilt.

Triadic complementary colours

TRIADIC COMPLEMENTARY

This uses three colours that are evenly spaced around the colour wheel. It can make for a bright and vibrant quilt.

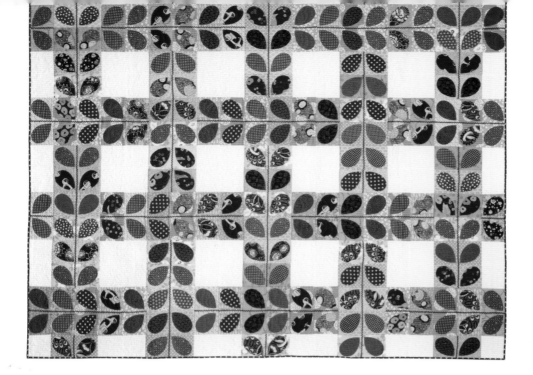

◀ *Brioni Greenberg's Primavera appliqué quilt (**Quilt Colour Workshop**) is a fantastic example of how using colour theory can result in an exciting quilt. It uses the triadic colour scheme, where the three colours used are evenly spaced on the colour wheel. The proportion of colour and repetition of the design means they compete with and complement each other in equal amounts, resulting in a vibrant effect, especially when placed on the crisp white background.*

COLOUR DEFINING TERMS

As well as the theories associated with using the colour wheel, there are other principles you may come across and want to consider when designing a quilt.

Temperature We often refer to colours as being hot and cold, and the wheel divides these up with reds and oranges on one side and blues and greens on the other. Some colours, such as violet, can be both depending on how much red or blue is in the colour.

Hue This refers to the colour, and when looking at secondary or tertiary colours, it will usually be the name of the most dominant colour. When working with fabric, considering this can be helpful to understand if a colour is, for example, a blue-violet (cool) or a red-violet (hot).

Value This refers to how light or dark a fabric is.

Intensity This refers to how bright the fabric is. Tints, tones and shades can all affect the intensity of a fabric. Noticing how intense the colour of a fabric is can help you select ones that sit comfortably next to each other.

Contrast When colours are placed next to one another they affect how the eye perceives them. For example, a red will stand out more if placed on green, its complementary colour, than on a purple, its adjacent colour. They will also be affected by the quantities of each colour.

Tint

Tone

Shade

Monochromatic

Tint This is a colour that has had white added to it. This can make a colour paler or softer looking, for example, quietening a red to look like a pink.

Tone This is a colour that has had grey added to it. It can reduce the intensity of a colour and make a palette look calmer. For example, a quilt made from primary colours (red, yellow and blue) can look quite child-like, but with the addition of a small amount of grey to each of these colours, the palette will have a more mature feel.

Do audition fabrics next to each other using the proportions you plan to use in your quilt to check that the colours work together in the way you have designed.

Shade This is a colour that has had black added to it. It can make a colour look more dramatic, although it reduces the intensity so it can look dull.

Monochromatic This refers to using tints and shades of the same colour for a harmonious look. In quilt making it can be used to make interesting colourwash effects where the fabric is graded from light to dark.

CREATING A COLOUR SCHEME

Here are some tips for creating a colour palette when selecting fabrics for your quilt making.

USE PHOTOGRAPHS

One of the easiest ways to create a colour scheme is to look at a photograph, then pull your palette from this image. Nature provides an endless source of inspiration, from tropical sunsets to snow-covered forests, while urban photographs can often surprise with unexpected colour combinations.

CREATE PAPER SWATCH CARDS

Starting with pages from magazines or paint reference cards from DIY stores, use paper scissors to cut swatches of colours that you like. Lay them out and mix and match until you have a palette that you are happy with. Stick your swatches onto index cards and refer to these when selecting fabrics, confident in the knowledge that you like the way they go together.

NAME YOUR COLOURS

Many fabric and thread companies name their colours rather than just giving them a number; browsing through their catalogues, you'll see how words such as 'tangerine' or 'slate' can spark a feeling. Take a selection of colours and think of a name for each beyond their basic hue: this will make you question what it is you like about a particular colour and what meaning it has to you.

PAINT A COLOUR WHEEL

One of the best ways to understand colours, particularly tints, tones and shades, is to mix different quantities of primary colour paints to make your own colour wheel. You then start to be able to look at a colour and see that it is, say, two thirds yellow, one third blue with some grey mixed in. Keep the colour wheel in your sketchbook to refer back to.

GATHER IDEAS

Keep notes on what colour schemes you have seen and liked. It can be as simple as spotting a shop logo or seeing tins displayed together in a supermarket. Explore the work of artists such as Sonia Delaunay, Wassily Kandinsky and Mark Rothko to see the interesting ways they have used colour in their work.

TAKE RISKS

Sometimes colours in a quilt can go together so well that they look a bit flat. Adding a small amount of something daring, that clashes or jars with the expected, can be what makes it work.

PHOTO CREDIT: Hornickrivlin.com

▲ The Sailor's Delight quilt designed by Debbie Grifka (**Quiltcon Magazine**) shows the result of using colour theory being used in an adept way. The overall design of the quilt is minimalist, with regular bands in two shades of blue placed on a white background. However, the choice of orange (it's complementary) as a highlight colour in the piecing and binding gives it a vibrancy, and means the smallest slithers of fabric carry a presence among the blue.

KEEP IT SIMPLE

When working with a complex quilt design, limiting your palette to just two colours can make the piecing the star of the show.

EXPLORE LIGHTS AND DARKS

It is important to consider your selection of colours as lights and darks as it can completely change the character of your quilt. If you want a bold geometric look, then go for a high contrast with lights and darks at each end of the scale. If you want a subtle effect with colour flickering across the quilt, then choose fabrics with low contrast. To view your colour selection as lights and darks, take a photograph then turn it into a black-and-white image.

Selecting colours exercise

While reading about colour helps to form ideas, handling swatches, looking at colours and making choices is where you can really start to understand the principles. This exercise uses fabric, but it could easily be done with paper, such as pages torn from a magazine.

1 Gather some fabric in a wide range of colours: this can be scraps, leftover charm squares or a sample pack (A).

2 Go through the colour wheel descriptions (see The Colour Wheel and Exploring Colour Options), selecting a combination of fabrics to go with each term (B). These fabrics were chosen for the colour wheel terms split complementary (left) and analogous (right).

3 Next, choose a random word. Think about your chosen word and what it means to you, then put together a colour palette that captures those thoughts (C). For example, the word 'rain' might bring to mind watery blues and reflections, leading on to grey clouds, or a fisherman's yellow raincoat and red wellington boots – see where your imagination will take you.

4 If you like the fabrics, take a photo, then put them back in the pile and repeat, this time choosing a new word (D). These fabrics were chosen for the word 'quiet'.

If your mind goes blank and you can't think of a word, open a book and select the first word on the page.

A

B

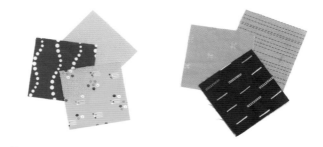

C

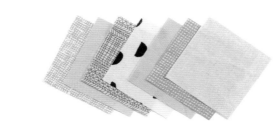

D

Image inspiration exercise

Explore how an image can be used to pull a colour scheme. This exercise ties in with our emotional response to colour. Take a photo or choose an image that resonates with you. There is no wrong or right: be guided by what you like from a vibrant sunset to a lush green landscape, or even a friend's living room – just look for a combination of colours that attracts you.

1 Choose an image or photograph that has the colours you wish to use in a quilt. If you can, enlarge the image so you can see more detail of the colour variations within it.

Using your own photographs for inspiration also gives a quilt added meaning as, even if a piece is abstract, the colours are based on a location or experience connected to your personal memories.

2 Take an old magazine or coloured paper and find colours that match those in your picture, tearing them out until you have ten pieces that represent the colours in your image or photograph (or as near as). From each one cut a small rectangle, then place them in a row. Put them in a rough order that matches how they are in your picture and glue them onto a piece of paper. If you want to take this further, this can be repeated with different layouts, cutting the swatches into squares and circles for example, to see how they will relate to one another.

3 To focus on a smaller range of colours, return to your image and look along one side only (if you prefer, you can trim a piece off to get a cross-section you like). Mark seven random dots in this area, trying to include many different hues, then tear these colours from the magazine/coloured paper and place together as before.

A

B

C

DESIGN DECISIONS

I find it hard to part with small pieces of fabric so always end up using them to make scrap quilts. When I designed this project, I had a pile of very small pieces of fabric from ranges designed by Alison Glass in my stash and wanted to get the most out of them, so rather than using a different fabric for the frame, I decided to trim them down first, which meant I could use them twice in the piece. This design was enjoyable to work on as despite the slow hand-stitching start, it quickly comes together on the machine at the end.

Project 1:
COLOUR CIRCLE WALL HANGING

I designed this wall hanging to explore colour choice. I have used lots of different coloured pre-cut squares, an easy way of sourcing a range of fabrics, but you could choose just one colour, graduating from light to dark. The ring is made by English paper piecing, with block piecing and quilting completed on the machine. The size is also suitable for a large cushion, or make a quilt by joining together four or nine blocks.

Finished size

20in square

You will need

› Twenty-four 5in squares, each a different colour
› One 5in grey square
› Four 9½in grey squares
› 24in square wadding (batting)
› 24in square backing fabric
› 7½in x WOF white binding fabric

NOTE: USE ¼IN SEAM ALLOWANCE QUANTITIES BASED ON FABRIC 42IN WIDE

1 Cut a 1½ x 3½in strip from each of the twenty-four different coloured 5in squares and set aside.

2 Using the template (see Templates), prepare twenty-four wedge shapes using the leftover fabric from step 1 (refer to Piecing: English Paper Piecing).

3 Lay out the prepared wedge shapes in a circle. Move them around till you are happy with their placement. If you are creating a colour wheel or graduated colour scheme, you may find it helpful to take a photo and convert it to a black-and-white image, so you just see the tones.

4 Sew the wedges together to make the four quarters of the circle (A). Take the quarters and sew them together to make two halves (B). Sew the halves together to make a circle (C). Give it a press, making sure the iron is not too hot as it can scorch the paper.

5 Take the four grey 9½in background squares and place them in a two by two arrangement. Sew them together into two rows of two, then sew the rows together.

6 Place the circle on the background using the seams of the squares to make sure it is positioned in the centre. When you are happy with its placement, pin it in place. Using slip stitch, sew the inner edge of the ring to the background. Use a stitch unpick to remove the tacking (basting) stitches, then carefully remove the backing papers along the outer edge of the ring, then slip stitch the outer edge to the background.

7 Now add the border to the quilt top. First, cut the 5in grey square into four 1½in squares. With the quilt top right side up on your work table, place the rectangles cut in step 1 around the outside, matching the colour of the rectangle to the colour of the wedge and placing a small grey square at each corner.

8 Sew the six rectangles for each side border together and sew onto the sides of the quilt top.

9 Sew the six rectangles and two end squares for the top and bottom borders together and sew onto the top and bottom of the quilt top.

10 Layer the backing, wadding (batting) and quilt top, then quilt as desired (refer to Finishing: Layering a Quilt and Quilting. I machine quilted a cross-hatch design using a pale grey thread.

11 Cut three 2¼in x WOF strips from the white fabric and join together, then use to bind the quilt using the double-fold binding method with mitred corners (refer to Finishing: Binding).

A

B

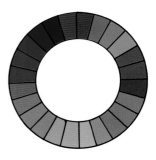

C

PHOTO CREDIT: Matt Graves

FABRIC

With its tactile qualities and wide range of types, print and colour, selecting fabric for a project is an immensely enjoyable part of the quilting process. When using fabric there are two different considerations. First, there are the technical issues, such as how to wash and press the fabric, and these are covered in Fabric Types. Second, there is working with designs, prints and ranges to achieve the look that you want for your quilt, which is the subject of this chapter.

◀ *Ombre fabrics can create really exciting visual effects, as seen on this detail from the colourful Melting Candy quilt by Gina Tell (**Modern Patchwork** magazine). In this twist on the traditional Log Cabin design, the blocks have been placed on-point (diagonally) and the colour change across the fabrics gives it an almost iridescent effect.*

CHOOSING FABRIC

There are many different types of fabric available for use in quilt making. Here is an overview of some of the ones most commonly seen.

PLAINS (ALSO KNOWN AS SOLIDS)

Plains are usually dyed and so have flat colour and are the same on each side. When only plains are used in a quilt they look modern and draw the viewer's attention to the design created by the piecing as there is nothing to distract from it, but they can also be used with prints to create a quiet space in a design. If you use lots of plains from a particular brand, look online to see if you can buy a shade card or pack of swatches. This makes it easy to order exactly what you want when buying online, especially if you are working to a specific colour palette.

PRINTS

The range of commercially printed fabric available to buy can be overwhelming, so look out for shops that specialise in fabrics for modern quilters as you will be able to browse a curated range. Whether you are using your choice of printed fabric to spark an idea for your quilt design, or selecting prints for an already planned project, remember that designers usually produce fabrics as part of a range, using a similar colour palette and theme with different prints and scales that will go together, so if you have chosen one fabric, do take a look to see what has been designed to go with it. When selecting fabric be aware of the scale of the print: large prints make excellent backings as you get to see the whole of the design, but the design of the print may get lost if you are working with small patches.

Look at the fabric selvedge to see what colours have been used to make the print and, for a coordinated look, match your other fabrics to these.

TWO-COLOUR FABRICS AND NEAR SOLIDS

These are mid-way between plains and prints and are really useful when making a modern quilt as you get the impact of a large single area of colour while having some printed detail to break up that area. They can be abstract with just a line or a scuff mark, or more figurative with text or a tiny print.

OMBRE

These fabrics graduate from light to dark, or from one colour to another. They can be used in strips to show colour washing across a quilt, or cut up and used to create areas of light and darks. They are a more inexpensive way of buying different colours: for example, you may need six different plains to give a graduated effect, but with an ombre you need cut up just one piece of fabric.

▲ *Zeena Shah is a print designer who works with different techniques such as mark making and screen printing. This detail of a fabric she has made for a bolster cushion (**How to Print Fabric**) is a graphic example of the modern effects that can be achieved by using simple tools, in this case the end of a foam brush.*

LOW-VOLUME FABRICS

The term 'low-volume' refers to mixing white and very pale fabrics that can be plain or printed. It results in a piece of patchwork that has slight variation in intensity but interest due to the subtle changes in prints and colour. If you are working on a quilt where a plain white is looking too stark, try replacing it with low-volume fabrics as the subtle changes in colour and print can give a softer look.

YARN-DYED FABRIC

This type of cloth is made from yarn that has been dyed before it has been woven. For quilting, look for a type that is woven in a regular way using two different colour threads for the weft and warp. This can initially look plain, but the colour changes slightly depending on the angle from which it is being viewed. This can be a good fabric to use instead of a plain when you are looking for a bit more interest or vibrancy but do not want the distraction of a print.

HAND-DYED FABRIC

You can buy these direct from dyers or produce your own. The range includes acid and procion dyed fabric, as well as those employing natural dyes such as indigo and onion skins. Hand-dyed fabric often has a flattish colour, although pattern can be added by using a technique such as wax resist or shibori (a form of tie dying).

HAND-PRINTED FABRIC

You can find textile designers who make hand-printed fabrics at events or online and using their work can give a unique finish to your project – as they are printing by hand their production runs will be a fraction of that of a large manufacturer, which means fewer quilters are able to use that particular fabric. The methods used to design the fabric, such as screen printing and block printing by hand, mean that they often have just two or three colours so can be used as a near solid. If you wish, you can also make your own fabric (see Print Your Own Fabric).

These print your own fabric samples include lino printed heart patches (below right), sun printing (top centre), stencilling with torn masking tape (top right) and screen printing (below left).

DIGITAL PRINTING

Digital printing is an option for creating a unique fabric to your own design. There are numerous online companies who provide the service, so it is easy to find a supplier. Simply scan your sketch or photograph into your computer, or create a design using design software, then upload it to the supplier's website, where you can reduce or enlarge it or try out different repeats until you are happy with how it looks. Once you have selected your cloth, which usually includes different weights of cotton and linen, and the quantity you would like, it is printed for you, usually arriving within a week or so. Many websites allow you to order as little as a fat quarter so you can see how your fabric will look before buying it in quantity.

PRINT YOUR OWN FABRIC

It can be extremely satisfying to print your own fabric and many of the ideas here require just fabric paint, a paintbrush or marking tool and your imagination. You can hand print straight onto fabric or onto scrap paper first, which could also be sent off to be digitally printed, so you get the look of an original print but can easily reorder as required.

STAMPING

Using items around the home to stamp with is a really easy way to make a print fabric. The end of pens, bubble wrap, cups, children's building bricks – all can be printed with, either by painting fabric paint directly onto the object or by stamping it into a fabric ink-pad or fabric paint that has been rolled out.

LINO PRINTING

This is a form of printing where you draw a design onto a piece of lino (or similar product), use a tool to cut away the surface and then apply fabric paint or ink on top to make a relief print. Supplies are inexpensive and can be bought from art shops.

STENCILLING

For this technique, simply cut your shape out of a piece of card or freezer paper, place it on the fabric and apply fabric paint or ink through the cut-out space with a brush, roller or sponge.

SCREEN PRINTING

A screen made from a silk mesh is placed on the fabric and a squeegee tool is used to scrape a thin layer of fabric paint or ink through it (the screen is prepared so ink can only go through at certain places). Often done in a professional printing studio, a version can be achieved at home using resists, such as freezer paper applied to the screen or by painting on a special screen-printing fluid.

THERMOFAX PRINTING

This uses old photocopier technology to make a small screen that can be used in the same way as screen printing. There are companies who provide this as a service, so you can email your design and get the screen back in the post.

TRANSFER PRINTING

For this form of printing, you draft your design onto paper using special paint or crayons, then place the paper pattern-side down onto the fabric and apply heat using an iron or heat press. This transfers the design onto the fabric. The nature of the dyes used means this technique works best with manmade fabrics such as polyester, although you can buy a product to pre-treat natural fibres such as cotton if you prefer.

SUN PRINTING

To create a sun print, apply a special fluid to your fabric, place an item on top (objects such as feathers, lace and layered threads all work well), then leave in the sun. The area that is covered by the object will lose the intensity of colour and the areas that are uncovered will become darker.

◀ Bold blocks make up the Dasher bathmat designed by Brioni Greenberg (**25 Ways to Sew Jelly Rolls, Layer Cakes and Charm Packs**). The centre of each of the Church Dash blocks has a fussy cut square as a focal point. These are bordered by a thin strip of the same purple fabric used in the negative space around the blocks which helps to create a sense of the blocks floating in the background.

Fussy cutting exercise

This is a technique where you select a specific piece of the print for your patch. It can either be used for focus, for example placing a motif in the centre of your square, or for playing with symmetry when you want lots of identical units, for example putting together a six-sided star. It can be wasteful but the visual effect from units cut from an identical part of the print can be stunning. This exercise gives an overview of the process.

1 Choose a fabric with a motif that you like – I chose a floral print from designer Amy Butler. Draw a square and triangle onto template plastic or card. Then draw another line ¼in away (or more if your seam allowance is more generous). Cut out the shape on the outer line, and if using card cut out the centre to make a window (A).

2 Place your chosen shape on your fabric, moving it to audition the part of the print you want (B). Be aware that the part of the motif in the seam allowance will not be seen in the finished design. When you are happy with the position of your template, either draw around it and cut the fabric using scissors, or carefully place your ruler on top and rotary cut.

3 If you want to make sure each patch has an identical part of the design, you can add registration lines that can be used to cut lots of patches exactly the same. Cut your shape from template plastic, then place it on the fabric and trace the design (C). Use these lines when cutting each patch to make sure they are all identical.

To make sewing easier, be aware of the grain when selecting areas to cut.

A

B

C

Project 2:
HIGHLIGHTER BOOK BAG

Smaller items such as bags and cushions are perfect for showing off fabric that has been printed at home. The pink linen I printed onto was lightweight and more suitable for dress making, so where it was used for the handles and bag outer, I made it firmer by applying medium-weight fusible interfacing to the reverse. I used the end of a highlighter pen to print my fabric but look around to see what you have to hand, or fashion your own stamping tool out of a piece of wire.

Finished size

14 x 16in (minus handles)

You will need

› 15in x WOF medium-weight blue denim
› 25in x WOF pink linen
› White fabric paint
› Printing tool
› Felt (optional)
› Pale pink perle 8 embroidery thread

NOTE: USE ¼IN SEAM ALLOWANCE
QUANTITIES BASED ON FABRIC 42IN WIDE

1 Cut your fabrics as follows:

From the pink linen:

› Two 5 x 16½in rectangles for the bag outer
› Two 2 x 25¾in strips for the handles
› Two 14½ x 16½in rectangles for the lining

From the blue denim:

› Two 10 x 16½in rectangles for the bag outer
› Two 2 x 25¾in strips for the handles

2 Set up your workspace for printing. Protect your work table with some newspaper or old fabric. You can lay some felt on top if you choose to as this will help the printing tool to sink into the fabric.

3 Place one of the pink bag outer rectangles on the work surface, taping the edges of the fabric so it stays in place if needed. Use a paintbrush to lightly cover your printing tool – in this case the bottom of a highlighter pen – with paint. Press the tool onto your fabric to create a print. Repeat to build up your design: I wanted mine to be evenly spaced in a straight line, so I placed my quilting ruler on the fabric and printed along the side of it.

4 Continue to print your design onto the second pink bag outer rectangle and the pink handle strips. When you have finished, allow your printed fabric to dry completely before going on to step 5.

5 Sew a pink and denim rectangle together to make one side of the bag. (To add interest to the denim fabric, I've sewn lines of running stitch 1¼in apart with the pale pink embroidery thread.)

6 Place the outer bag pieces right sides together. Sew up the sides and along the bottom and turn right side out.

7 Now make the handles. Take a denim strip and a pink printed strip, place them right sides together and sew down the sides. Turn right side out. Repeat to make the second handle strap. Press, then topstitch along each strap approximately ⅛in from the edge.

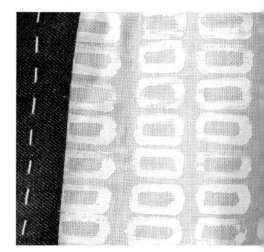

8 Take a handle strap and place one end at the top edge of the bag about 2½in from the left-hand side seam, so that the raw edges of the strap and the bag are aligned; pin in place. Repeat to pin the other end of the handle strap the same distance away from the right-hand side seam, making sure that the handle is not twisted. Sew the handles in place close to the edge (so the stitching will be hidden in the seam allowance). Repeat to fix the remaining handle strap on the other side of the bag.

9 Place the two lining pieces wrong sides together, then stitch down the sides and along the bottom, leaving a gap of approximately 7in at the centre of the bottom edge.

10 Place the bag outer inside the lining with right sides together. Align the top edges making sure the side seams are aligned then pin. Sew around the top, then turn the bag right side out through the gap in the lining and ease out the corners. Sew the gap in the lining closed then push the lining into the bag.

11 To finish, topstitch about ⅛in from the edge all the way around the top of the bag.

COMPOSITIONAL ELEMENTS

When designing a modern quilt there are a number of design principles to take into consideration. Negative space, and symmetry and asymmetry are widely used, so these are covered in their own chapters, but other important themes such as balance and minimalism are discussed here. Whether you choose to closely follow or ignore the principles, an awareness of them helps when planning and putting together a design.

▲ *Katie Clark Blakesley's Cut Glass Baby quilt (**Vintage Quilt Revival**) is a great example of the rule of thirds being used in a quilt design. The graphic piecing and modern colours really pop, but the addition of the detail block (bottom right) gives the quilt a focal point and keeps the viewer exploring the shapes for longer than they would have, had each block been identical.*

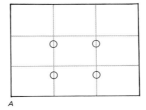

◀ *The Hexagon Star quilt by Pam and Nicky Lintott is from **New Ways with Jelly Rolls**, a book which features reversible modern quilts. With the use of quick techniques such as improv and oversized blocks, the back of a quilt is often as important as the front, presenting an opportunity for developing a new design as well as being a practical way to use up leftover fabric. Here, just three units have been positioned off-centre on the back of the quilt, giving a minimalistic feel. Interior designers will often group objects in threes (or odd numbers) as it is considered to be the most pleasing to the eye.*

MINIMALISM

A minimalist piece of work is about simplicity and allowing space for the viewer to form their own idea. It can be seen in traditional quilts, such as wholecloths, but is very common in modern quilting where using a simple design creates a big impact. When making a quilt, minimalism means taking it down to the bare elements of design and using the fabric and stitch in a considered way to achieve this. With less happening, what is left carries heavier meaning, so take time to achieve a balance to the composition.

PROPORTION, SCALE AND BALANCE

Although often referred to together, these terms mean different things and getting them right can sometimes be difficult to achieve, and you may find that your design needs tweaking to make it work.

If a design is 'in proportion' then the elements relate to one another in a harmonious way. If the boundaries of proportion are pushed, such as an oversized chair with a tiny cushion, then it can create something that looks surreal. It is often easy to spot something that is not in proportion, a tiny picture placed singularly on a large wall for example; but it may be that a deliberate decision has been made to present it that way, a priceless masterpiece placed solo to define its importance. The same can be done in modern quilting by placing a tiny block within a large border.

Generally, scale refers to size and this will be either the shapes used within a quilt or the overall dimensions. A common way scale is altered in modern quilting is with oversized blocks. Many traditional blocks are around 12in square, but in modern quilting these can be supersized, up to 60in square and larger.

Balance refers to how the design elements sit together and work alongside each other. In quilt making, this can refer not only to the shapes, but to how the style of the fabric prints and colours relate to one another when they are put together.

RULE OF THIRDS

Used by graphic designers, photographers and filmmakers, the rule of thirds refers to positioning objects within a grid separated by two evenly spaced horizontal and vertical lines. The frame can be a square or a rectangle (A), or another shape, such as a circle. You may already be aware of these lines as some cameras automatically show them in the viewfinder when you take a photo. An example of how this is used can be seen in landscape photography where the horizon is often positioned along one of the horizontal lines. In quilt design, this can be used in instances where one block is a different colour to the rest or the quilting pattern is different in one area. If you are designing a quilt with a focal block, or a minimalist quilt with a single block surrounded by background fabric, then try placing it where the grid intersects and see if you like where it sits.

A

FIBONACCI

This mathematical theory is intriguing for quilters. The basic idea is simple, that the next number in the sequence equals the sum of the previous two numbers, so, if we start with 1, the next number is 1, then the next is 2, 3, 5, 8, and so on. The pattern is widely seen in nature. For quilt design purposes, this theory can be used with lines, squares or to make a spiral and it makes an interesting rule to experiment with.

LINES

These can seem almost an afterthought but can be very strong in design terms. Just look at sketches by fashion illustrators; with just a few lines they can draw not only a figure but give it expression and a sense of movement. In quilt design, lines can connect and/or separate areas. They can be thick or thin, long or short, straight or curved, dashed or continuous, to draw the viewer's eye and affect proportion. If you are working on a minimalist quilt, a well-positioned line can be the thing that holds the parts of the design together.

Proportion exercise

This is a quick process that explores proportion and balance so you can determine what you like and question why this is. Try it several times with different coloured paper or card to see how the colour affects the result.

1 Cut the following from four different coloured papers or pieces of card:

› **Two 2in squares**
› **Four 3in squares**
› **Three 6in squares**

2 Start with an easy composition. Pick a 3in square at random and place it in the centre of a different coloured 6in square (A). Glue in place.

3 Take three 2in squares and place them on top of a 6in square. Consider how the distance between the shapes changes the feel of the composition, and move them around, rotating them if you wish, until you achieve a design you are happy with (B). Glue in position.

4 Take two 3in squares and place them on top of a 6in square. Unless you want them to go right to the edge they will need to be overlapped (C); move them around so they are in a design that you feel comfortable with. Glue in position.

5 Continue to make small compositions to use the remaining papers, cutting more squares as required, using the process to explore how the distance between the shapes and how they overlap affects the way each arrangement looks (D–L).

If you enjoyed making these compositions, they could be used to plan a quilt design, or to create a series of small, stitched collage (appliquéd) quilts.

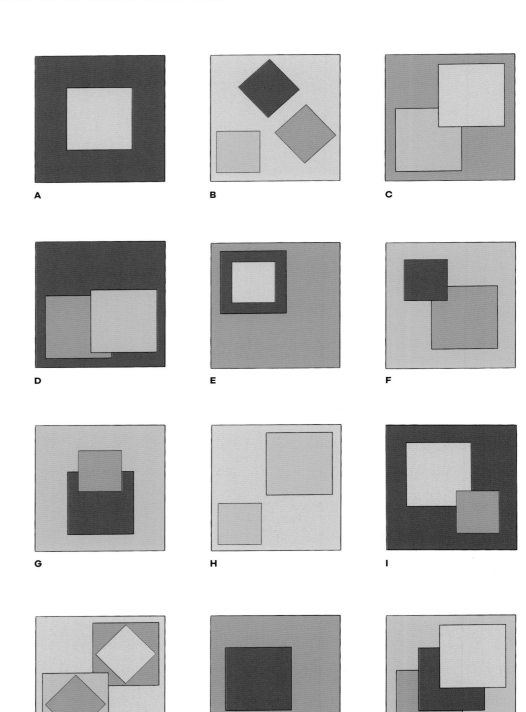

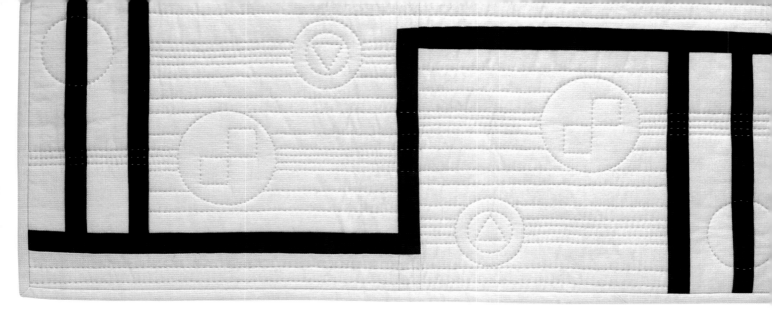

PHOTO CREDIT: Kim Sayer and Karl Adamson

Lines exercise

This is one of my favourite exercises to do when I am stuck for a quilting idea. Doodling is the quilter's friend as in theory each line could be translated into a line of quilting stitch. Although I've used pen on paper, this exercise works well on a tablet too, and apps are available to enable you to save the designs to flick through next time you need inspiration.

▲ *This table runner by Julia Davis and Anne Muxworthy (**Easy Japanese Quilt Style**) is an excellent example of the visual power that a couple of well-placed lines can have when making a piece with a minimalist feel. The overall look is understated, with just two colours contrasting. The hand quilting design adds texture and interest with shapes, but the choice of thread colour means it does not compete with the graphic effect of the piecing.*

1 Gather together a selection of pens with different size nibs. Take a piece of white paper and draw nine same-sized squares. In each square draw three lines in different arrangements to create minimalist compositions (A). You can repeat the exercise drawing five lines in different arrangements, then seven, and so on.

2 Now take a sheet of lined paper (or draw horizontal lines onto a piece of plain paper). Along each space draw a different line, thick, thin, dashed, curved, whatever you like, but try to make each one different (B).

3 Take another piece of white paper and draw nine same-sized squares as in step 1, but this time rather than draw straight lines in each, choose some you like from step 2, such as a wide zigzag perhaps, and develop further (C). Now review your work. Which ones would you like to develop further?

A

C

B

Project 3:

SNIPPETS COASTERS

This is a quick and easy make and perfect for using up odd pieces of fabric and wadding (batting) leftover from a previous project. It is inspired by the Fibonacci formula which has been drawn onto paper and used as a template for the quilting lines – but alternatively you could make these using some of your line designs from the Lines Exercise.

Finished size

4½in square each coaster

You will need:

› Four 4¾in squares for the coaster fronts

› Four 5in squares for the coaster backs

› Four 5in squares wadding (batting)

› Four 2½ x 30in strips, each a different fabric, for binding

1 Take a piece of paper that measures about 10 x 15in. If you need to tape two smaller pieces together that is fine as it is just a template. Near the centre draw a line across the width. Next draw another line ¼in away from the central line on each side. Draw another line ½in away from the central line on each side. Continue drawing lines each side of the central line with the distance of the measurement being the sum of the previous two lines (A).

2 Take one of the 4¾in squares of fabric and place it on top of the paper, anywhere you like. Using a ruler and fabric-marking pen (I used a water-soluble pen) trace the lines onto the fabric (B). Repeat with the other three 4¾in squares, placing them in different positions on the paper to make a slightly different design on each.

3 Place a square of wadding (batting) on the wrong side of a 5in square of fabric. Then place one of the marked squares on top, right side facing up, and pin together if necessary. Repeat to prepare the other three coasters.

4 Put a walking foot (if you have one) on your sewing machine and set to a slightly longer stitch length. Choose a coaster and a line at random and sew along it. Start and finish each line of stitching in the wadding (batting) so that you don't need to secure the ends. Trim excess threads as you go so they don't get tangled. Sew along all the lines, changing the thread colour as you wish. When you have finished, trim each coaster to 4½in square.

5 To prepare the binding, cut 1½in off the end of each strip. Trim each strip to about 12–15in from the start and sew in a contrast 1½in strip.

6 Stitch the binding to each coaster using the double-fold binding method with mitred corners (see Finishing: Binding). Before starting, place the binding on the fabric and work your way around the side to make sure the contrast strip does not fall at a corner as the extra bulk for the seam allowance can make it difficult to achieve a neat mitre.

If you enjoy making these coasters, you can adapt the design to sew a set of matching placemats.

A

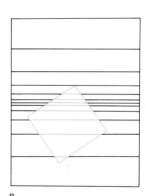

B

GRIDS

A grid is a series of lines that cross or intersect each other. The lines can be square or diagonal, with regular or irregular spacing. Grids can be seen everywhere in our daily lives, from maps showing the way city planners have laid out streets, to how architects design the front of buildings – even this page will have started with a graphic designer laying out text and images according to a grid. Depending on how they are used, grids can bring order and control to a design or give a chaotic feel.

▲ *Lucie Summers' vibrant Building Blocks quilt (**Quilt Improv**) has lots happening in terms of shape and colour. The grid has been broken down to be regular in some areas and irregular in others, encouraging your eye to quickly dart around the piece. The carefully selected fabrics, a combination of prints and plain, bring it all together as there are places for your eye to rest.*

◄ *If you prefer to work in a spontaneous way, the thought of using a grid in your design can feel constrained. However, a grid can be a useful tool when putting together blocks, and as shown in Coleen Merte's Pink Grapefruit quilt (**Quiltmaker magazine**) it can create the space to experiment with design concepts when piecing and quilting. Here, the thought given to the negative space has resulted in an exciting and dynamic piece of work, with the viewer's eye taken on journey from the top left corner to the bottom right. Added to this, the play on symmetry within the grid, such as areas where the curves are missing from the sides of the blocks, add a huge amount of visual interest.*

GRIDS IN QUILT MAKING

In quilt making the most widely seen design is a basic grid, with a series of regular horizontal and vertical lines breaking up areas of patchwork. Traditional samplers are laid out in this way, hence the popularity of square blocks. In modern quilt design, this grid is often altered to create intriguing designs where the layout plays around with scale and proportion. Whether you choose to reject the grid layout or stick rigidly to one will be affected by principles such as proportion and symmetry, so do review the Compositional Elements and the Symmetry and Asymmetry chapters.

When designing a quilt, a regular grid can be a good place to start as it provides a guide of areas to fill in with piecing or appliqué, and as the grid is predictable, it means the focus is on other areas of design, such as the fabric prints or the texture created by the quilting. Following the principles of symmetry, a regular grid tends to be easy on the eye. It also makes it easier to work out measurements for the finished quilt size as all you need to do is multiply the number of blocks by the finished size of each block. Grids can also be used when quilting and the stitching designed as a grid to be placed on top of the quilt.

Designing a grid with an irregular layout can be a little more work but the results can be worth it as it makes the viewer's eye work a little harder. The irregularity can be as simple as planning in advance to have blocks that are all square but different sizes, such as 4in, 8in, 12in and 16in, or you can work intuitively to make blocks, then resolve how to fit them together with the addition of filler fabric pieces or trim them down.

Grids play an important role in quilt making when planning a piece of work. Even if a design is abstract, adding a grid on top at the planning stage breaks down the design into something that has a structured working method for assembly. It enables you to work out what sections can be put together easily, then to plan how they will fit together. Sometimes, for example, you can make several sections, then to join them you have a couple of tight corners where partial seams are required to connect the whole piece together.

If you imagine two grids of squares drawn on tracing paper, placed on top of one another but not aligned, you start to see secondary areas, especially as you move them around. In quilt design this can be as simple as pieced squares with quilted squares, which have their own grid, on top. This idea can be taken further with varying scales and designs of grids containing different shapes placed on top of one another.

Altering grids exercise

If you like working with traditional blocks, this can be a good exercise for thinking up new layouts. You can work on paper with a ruler, pencil and eraser, or on an iPad or computer if you prefer. Consider how the distance between the lines and the spaces created by the lines change the look and feel of the grid. Also, try rotating grids by 90 or 180 degrees in steps 3–5 to see how they look. You may be surprised to discover how a grid that looks a little dull can suddenly look interesting when turned upside down.

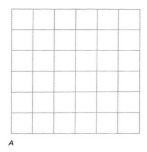

A

1 Draw a regular grid, with seven evenly spaced horizontal and vertical lines (A). Photocopy or trace this grid six times.

2 Take two copies and draw into the grids at regular intervals (B, C).

3 Take another two of the copies and draw into the grid at irregular intervals but keep the regular grid lines (D, E). This keeps the regular grid format but breaks it up.

4 Take the last two copies and draw different shapes into each box (F, G). This keeps the regular grid format but breaks it up in a more complex way.

5 Take the original pencil grid and use an eraser to remove some of the lines (H). This is completely breaking up the regular grid format

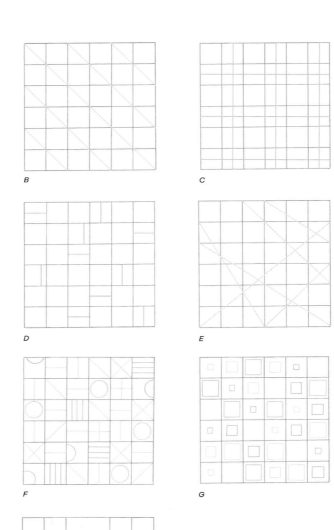

B

C

D

E

F

G

H

Working on paper, graph, squared or dot grid paper makes the job of drawing grids easier as they are already marked.

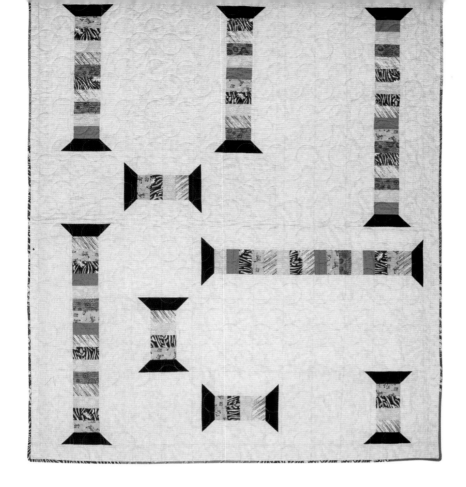

*◄ Pam and Nicky Lintott's Cotton Reels quilt (**New Ways with Jelly Rolls**) has rejected regular grid format to create a quilt that has movement with different areas of interest. Although the layout looks complex, the designers have cleverly broken it down into areas so the piecing is logical with no inset (partial) seams required. The use of negative space ensures that the reels are the focal point and its proportion gives it a calming feel.*

Irregular grid exercise

This exercise explores designing an irregular grid around blocks and it's a great way of using up stray blocks to create a cohesive piece. Choose the background fabric wisely as this can affect the overall look of the piece when used in a large quantity.

1 Measure your blocks and decide how you want to lay them out (in a row, randomly, etc.) then draw them onto graph, squared or dot grid paper (A). Use a ratio, for example, one square on the paper equals 1in.

2 Work out how large you want the quilt to be, then draw a border to mark the edges of the quilt (B).

3 Working methodically, start to fill in spaces around the blocks to plan the filler pieces of fabric (C). You can repeat this several times to find the most logical way for you to assemble the blocks into a quilt top.

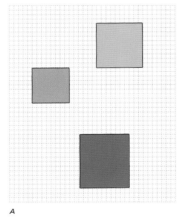

A

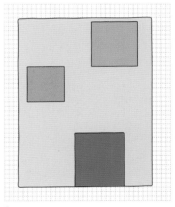

B

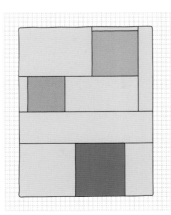

C

Project 4:
SUMMER SOLSTICE CUSHION COVER

I made this cushion cover using improv techniques, but to make sure it went together, the grid was planned beforehand. I have provided my guidelines but do give it your personal take (see Piecing: Improv Piecing). The beauty of improv is that if something does not look right or it comes up short, you can keep cutting into it or adding pieces onto it until you get the look you want. As I added a lot of quilting, my cushion panel shrunk, so ended up slightly smaller. If yours does the same, adjust the width of the envelope back pieces – the inner will still fit and look plump.

Finished size

18in square approx

You will need

› Selection of fabric for the front
› Fabric for the cushion back approx 15in x WOF
› 20in square wadding (batting)
› 20in square fabric to back wadding (batting)
› 18in square cushion inner

NOTE: USE ¼IN SEAM ALLOWANCE QUANTITIES BASED ON FABRIC 42IN WIDE

1 To make a rough plan of the pieces of improv you need to make, take a piece of graph, squared or dot grid paper and draw a square. Divide it up into sections. If you want to copy my layout the sizes are below. Use these sizes as a guide when making the improv units (these measurements include seam allowance).

› Block A 10½in square
› Block B 10½ x 2½in
› Block C 10½ x 6½in
› Block D 8½ x 4in
› Block E 8½ x 8in
› Block F 8½ x 7½in

2 Make the units. Block A and E use the quarter circle method, Block C uses strips, then Blocks D and F were assembled from the off-cuts (refer to Piecing: Improv Piecing). Block B is a single piece of fabric, but it could be pieced if you prefer. (For general advice on piecing, see Quilt Basics:

Piecing.) Once the units are made and cut to the required size, join them into two columns then sew them together (A).

3 Press the pieced panel. Layer the 20in fabric square, wadding (batting) and pieced panel, then quilt as desired (refer to Finishing: Layering a Quilt and Quilting). I machine quilted random lines in the different areas, then added in some hand quilting including a few cross stitches using perle 8 thread in assorted colours and a chenille size 22 needle.

4 When the quilting is finished, cut the backing and wadding (batting) level with the edge of the cushion front.

5 From the fabric for the back of the cushion, cut two pieces each measuring 18½ x 14in. On one long edge of each piece, turn under ½in and press. Then fold over another ½in and press to make a double turned hem, and stitch with a toning thread.

6 To make the envelope back, place the cushion front right side up onto your work surface. Take one of the back pieces and place it on the cushion front, right sides together, aligning the raw edges; pin in place (B). Repeat with the second back piece. The hemmed edges should overlap (C). Sew around the edge. Trim the excess fabric at the corners, turn through to the right side and press. Insert the cushion inner.

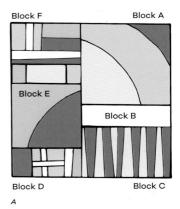

Block F   Block A

Block E

Block B

Block D   Block C

A

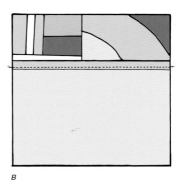

B

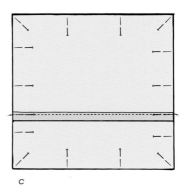

C

NEGATIVE SPACE

Negative space is the term given to the area that surrounds a shape (or shapes) and can be seen around the edge as well as in the gaps. It is used as a design tool across all the arts, from the styling of interiors to stage craft in the theatre. By placing as much importance on the background as on the areas of interest the whole composition is considered and planned. When planning a quilt, being aware of the negative space helps to control how specific areas of the design are viewed.

▲ *Negative space can be used to create movement, as shown on the Paint Drips quilt (Angela Pingel, **A Quilter's Mixology**). The use of the background fabric at the top of the quilt, as well as the standalone single circle 'drip', transmits the idea of motion. The wide band of background fabric at the bottom of the quilt gives a good sense of proportion, to make it really look as if the colours are running down a wall.*

▲ *The 42 Hashtags quilt by Tanya Finken (**Easy Quilts magazine**) is made from small (4 ½in square) blocks made from an ebullient range of colours that flow from one side of the quilt to the other. The choice of the pale fabric for the negative space complements the range of different colours and brings the blocks and oversized border together to make a cohesive eye-catching quilt.*

NEGATIVE SPACE IN QUILT MAKING

In traditional quilting, negative space is generally used to frame patchwork in a symmetrical way, for example with sashing strips between blocks. In modern quilting, however, negative space becomes an important part of the design to control the areas of interest, sometimes forming the initial quilt idea itself. It is also a useful tool to experiment with symmetry/asymmetry and alternative grid formats. For example, a quilt can be made from identical blocks, but if the fabric used blends into the border it can create the impression of an irregular layout, as can be seen in Project 5, the Night Sky Quilt.

When looking at a quilt the viewer's eye can initially be attracted to the blocks or printed fabric, but by making the negative space an important part of the design it encourages the viewer to look around the piece. This means colour is an important choice to make when considering the effect negative space has on a design. Strong contrast can bring the focal areas forward, while less of a contrast pushes them into the background. Depending on how the principles of colour – tints, tones, shades, etc. – are used, this can produce very different results and is something to be experimented with (see Quilt Design Exercise).

It is important to remember that negative space is the whole area behind the design, so not just the border. It can include all the smaller sections in the middle of the design and these create areas of space. An easy way to think about this is to take a really good look at some objects, such as picture frames and vases on a shelf. Observe the shapes created by the objects themselves and then the shapes in the gaps between and around them. Negative space is not just the area around the outside of these objects, it's also the space in the smaller gaps between them, in this case where they may overlap, and these shapes relate to the background.

Imagine the same idea with pieces of fabric in a quilt. Just because a shape is in the middle of the design does not mean this cannot be part of the negative space. In the Night Sky Quilt, navy fabric is used within the blocks as well as around the edge, to give a floating effect that makes the stars burst out from the background. It is these little areas of negative space that can be the most interesting to look at as they create space and can be used to accentuate a shape or to pull it into the main design.

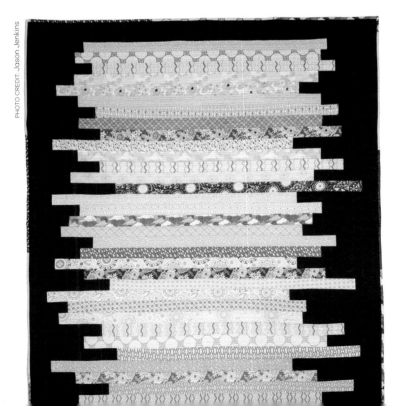

◀ *On the Skyline quilt (Pam and Nicky Lintott, **Jelly Roll Quilts in a Weekend**), the simple but clever use of negative space around the edge of the strips makes the viewer's eye travel around the quilt, up one side and then down the other. It is a good example of how choosing the correct colour and balance of contrast can make the focus fabric look as if it is projected out from the background.*

◄ *Here is a detail from the Pop Rocks quilt by Kacia Hosmer (**Modern Patchwork magazine**), which is a superb example of how negative space can be used to accentuate changes of scale and colour. The white negative space is interrupted every so often by the calming grey triangles adding interest to the background, then the varying size and positioning of the vibrant colour triangles appear to dance across the quilt.*

Drawing exercise

This simple exercise creates a positive and a negative image of an object or group of objects and is a good way to get your brain to think about shapes in the background rather than just the shape of the object(s).

1 Choose an object or a group of objects, something that you will find easy to draw (I like bottles and vases, or for a stitch theme you could use your sewing machine) and place on your work surface.

2 Now, taking no more than five minutes, draw the outlines of your chosen objects using a pencil or pen, and shade or colour them in (A).

3 Repeat the exercise, but this time draw just the background to the objects, shading and colouring in (B). Try not to draw the outline of the objects, but focus on the space behind and around them.

4 Now try step 3 with different objects, or just move the objects you used before to see how small changes in the background gaps result in a different look.

A

B

Quilt design exercise

This exercise is fairly quick to do and helps you to focus on the spaces around and between shapes. There are two different ways to do this: the first is to start with the areas of interest, then add in the negative space; the second is to start with the negative space, then add in the areas of interest. There are two exercises for each method, and the process will help you decide which approach you prefer.

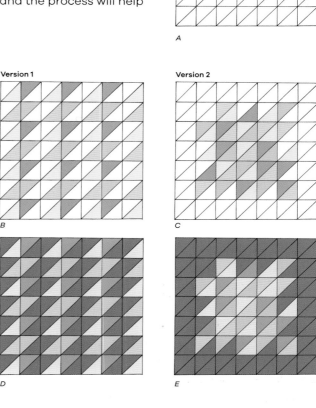

A

1 Draw an outline of a simple quilt. It can be anything you wish, perhaps one you have previously made of a single block layout, such as half-square triangles (A). Make four copies. Select four pens or pencils for your focus fabrics and one to represent the negative space in your design.

2 Place the colour for the negative space to one side. Then use your focus fabric pens to colour in two copies of your simple quilt outline as follows:

Version 1 Colour in rows or columns, leaving a regular gap in each row for the negative space (B).

Version 2 Colour in an area of the quilt – try to make the outline of this irregular (C).

3 Now colour in the negative space in each design (D, E).

4 Take the two remaining copies and the negative space pen and this time:

Version 3 Colour in from the outside in, leaving space for the focus colours (F).

Version 4 Colour various points, leaving space for the odd focus colour (G).

5 Now colour in the gaps in each design using the focus colours (H, I).

6 Consider whether you like more or less negative space in your design and remember, neither is right or wrong as it all comes down to personal preference.

If you are considering making your designs into a quilt, think about adding a border (which can be symmetrical or asymmetrical) to extend the amount of negative space.

Version 1

Version 2

B

C

D

E

Version 3

Version 4

F

G

H

I

DESIGN DECISIONS

When selecting fabric for a quilt where the design is heavily influenced by negative space, the first decision is invariably what colour this will be. This is the opposite to how I often work, which is to choose the focus fabrics first. With this quilt I wanted a dark background and chose navy as it is dramatic and works well with lots of different colours. When working on a quilt where the negative space is important, I will often choose a darker fabric as the seams are less visible; where two of the same fabrics are sewn together it creates a texture, which can catch the light and so create a shadow.

Project 5:
NIGHT SKY QUILT

This quilt is based on a traditional block, but play on scale and negative space make it modern. I enjoy the repetitive process of making block quilts, and often use the same fabric within the blocks to create smaller negative spaces, as well as for the sashing and borders (if it has them), to give the effect of the focus fabrics floating on top of the background fabric.

Finished size

67½in square approx

You will need

› 4½yd x WOF navy fabric
› 28in x WOF pink fabric
› 23in x WOF peach fabric
› 72in square backing fabric
› 72in square wadding (batting)

NOTE: USE ¼IN SEAM ALLOWANCE QUANTITIES BASED ON FABRIC 42IN WIDE

1 Cut your fabrics as follows:

From the navy fabric:

› Two 24in squares cut twice on the diagonal (for the sides)
› Four 16½in squares
› Two 12¼in squares cut once on the diagonal (for the corners)
› Four 2¼in x WOF strips for the binding
› Fifty-four 4½in squares for the blocks
› Forty-five 5¼in squares for the blocks

From the pink fabric:

› Twenty-seven 5¼in squares for the blocks
› Two 2¼in x WOF strips for the binding

From the peach fabric:

› Eighteen 5¼in squares for the blocks
› Two 2¼in x WOF strips for the binding

It is most economical to cut the large navy pieces first, cutting the smaller squares from the remaining fabric.

2 Match three pink squares and two peach squares with navy 5¼in squares and make half-square triangles (see Piecing: Triangles – Making Two HST Units at a Time). Press and trim units to 4½in square.

3 Lay out the HST units plus six navy 4½in squares (A). Sew the pieces together into rows, then sew the rows together (B). The finished block should measure 16½in square.

4 Repeat steps 2 and 3 to make a total of nine blocks.

5 Lay out the blocks, placing a navy 16½in square between each one and the navy filler triangles at the sides and corners (C). Join the pieces together to make diagonal rows, press, then sew the rows together (refer to Setting Triangles: Assembling Your Quilt in Piecing: Finishing a Design On-Point).

6 Press the quilt top and remove any stray threads. Layer the backing, wadding (batting) and quilt top, then quilt as desired (refer to Finishing: Layering a Quilt and Quilting); mine was long-arm quilted with an elongated figure of eight. Square up the quilt, making sure you trim ¼in away from the outer points of the filler triangles.

7 The binding is lapped, with two sides navy, one pink and one peach to give an asymmetric finish. Prepare the binding strips by sewing same colour strips together end to end in pairs. Fold each strip in half lengthways, wrong sides together, and press. Use the prepared binding strips to sew a double-fold binding with straight corners (refer to Finishing: Binding).

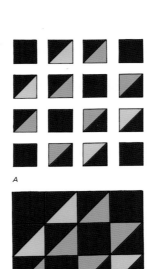

A

B

C

SYMMETRY AND ASYMMETRY

Playing around with symmetry is a design technique widely used in modern quilts. A perfect balance of symmetry is neat and ordered – our eyes presume how the overall design will look and this gives a sense of security. With asymmetry, however, there is no automatic logic to how something is balanced, so our eyes need to work a little bit harder to make sense of what is seen. When used in quilt design, these principles can be used to control how the viewer perceives the piece.

▲ *The asymmetry of the placement of the flowers combined with the vivid colour scheme gives Sandy Maxfield's Curvy Dogwood quilt (**Modern Quilting magazine**) strong visual impact. The flower blocks are positioned towards one side of the quilt but the curved strip down the side keeps the composition balanced and adds interest.*

TYPES OF SYMMETRY

There are several different types of symmetry, each of which can be applied in a different way when designing quilts.

Mirrored (reflective) symmetry This has a single line of axis where the image is the same on each side of it: think of the butterfly paintings you did as a child, where the paint is placed on one side of the paper, then folded in half and opened to give two sides with an equal design. In quilt making, this would be a block where the two halves have identical shapes and colours.

Rotational symmetry This refers to a shape that can be rotated around a central point and looks the same on each side. An example of this is an equilateral triangle, which can also be divided into three equal parts. Many English paper-pieced designs are developed from this form of rotational symmetry, for example sewing equilateral triangles together to form a hexagon.

Point symmetry This is where the design radiates out from a central axis like the ripples created by a raindrop on water. This can be seen in blocks such as Courthouse Steps, with each 'round' made from identical fabrics.

Translational symmetry This is where shapes move evenly apart. In modern quilt making, it can be combined with grids and negative space to achieve what initially appears to be an irregular layout, but where translational symmetry creates a rule to be followed. An example of this is a half-square triangle quilt where the colours reverse at specific points.

▲ *On Juliet van der Heijden's Night Owl quilt (**Animal Quilts**) the owl looks wonderfully dramatic swooping down from a black background. With a plain background there is nothing to distract from the foundation pieced bird, so it is the star of the show, and by being positioned asymmetrically in the bottom left-hand corner, it has been given movement as if it is in flight.*

▲ *This table mat by Karen Lewis (**Wabi-Sabi Sewing**) shows how just a slight play with symmetry can result in an intriguing design. Here one unit has been placed to the side and a contrast fabric introduced, interrupting the flow of the layout which results in a quirky look.*

WORKING WITH ASYMMETRY

If the rules of symmetry create a sense of calm and order, asymmetry (where there is no axis of symmetry) can generate the opposite effect. The look can be unexpected and often provokes curiosity from the viewer. Working with asymmetry is all about pushing the rules, such as sewing a skirt with a hem that is above the knee on one side and skimming the ankle on the other. When using asymmetry in quilt making, it can interrupt the viewer's eye and draw attention to a particular point. An asymmetric quilt can still be a balanced design, however, for example by carefully selecting shapes that work together, in the same way that lots of different sizes and frames of photographs can be effectively combined on a wall. When planning an asymmetric design refer to the topics covered in the Compositional Elements chapter as the principles of themes such as balance and proportion are important to be aware of.

Often a tiny tweak can make a symmetrical quilt design appear to be asymmetrical, for example just changing the colour in one area can break up the pattern. This is a safe way to explore asymmetry as the piecing remains the same all over, and it is just the fabric colour or print that causes the interruption, drawing the viewer's attention to that element of the design. This can work particularly well if creating quilts with modern traditionalism (see Modern Traditionalism). Techniques such as forms of improvisational piecing (see Piecing: Improv Piecing) can force you to work in an asymmetric way, as it is difficult to control the scale to create identical pieced sections.

◀ The Nine-Patch Sunburst quilt (Pam and Nicky Lintott, **Jelly Roll Quilts in a Weekend**) has been made from half-square triangles pieced from pale spot and vibrant fabrics. While the piecing looks simple, the four-fold symmetry means there is a lot happening. The viewer's eye moves to see a star shape in the centre, the horizontal and vertical lines, then the diagonal lines. The effect is impressive and the regularity of the symmetry controls the many prints used.

Flying geese exercise

This exercise will help you to see whether you prefer symmetry or asymmetry in quilt design, working with popular flying geese blocks (see Piecing: Triangles).

1 On dot grid or graph paper, draw a grid of 1 x 2in rectangles (A). Copy or trace it to give you four copies.

2 On two of the copies, draw a design of flying geese that are symmetrical and colour them in (B, C).

3 Repeat step 2 with the remaining two copies, but this time make an asymmetrical design (D, E).

4 Review the designs close up and at a distance. Do you feel more comfortable with the symmetrical designs, or do you prefer the intrigue of the asymmetrical ones?

B

C

A

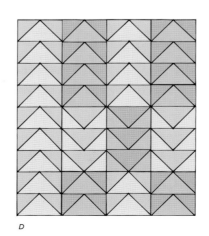

D

E

Borders exercise

This task gives you the opportunity to question if you like asymmetric borders, and if so what scale you prefer, and how the piecing can affect the look.

1 Draw two quilt centres, one with large squares (A), the other with small squares (B). Make three copies of each and colour them in.

2 Now draw an equal border around each side of one set and colour them in (C, D).

3 On the remaining sets, draw and colour in two asymmetric borders around the centres with one slightly out (E, F) and the other very pronounced (G, H).

As they use basic shapes, the designs in these exercises make a good basis for quick quilts.

A

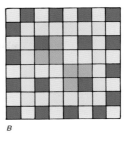

B

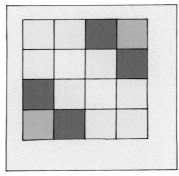

C

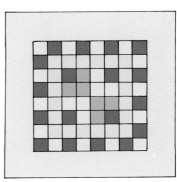

D

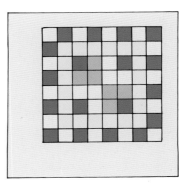

E

F

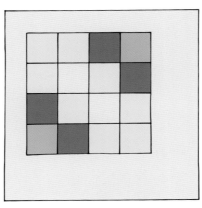

G

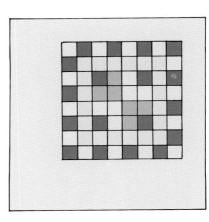

H

Project 6:
THROUGH THE WINDOW QUILT

The pieced panel in the centre of this quilt is based on the traditional Log Cabin block with the strips added methodically around a centre square. However, I experimented with a few slightly wonky lines in the piecing then laid the blocks out in an irregular grid format, so there is an element of control amongst the chaos. The white fabric has been used to create an interesting amount of negative space, with it being used in the blocks as well as the asymmetric border. The finished piece reminds me of looking out of a misted window on a sunny but snowy winter's day.

Finished size

53¼in square approx

You will need

› 3yd x WOF plain white fabric
› A total of 7½ x WOF assorted grey print fabrics
› A total of 9½ x WOF assorted yellow print fabrics
› A total of 7½ x WOF assorted black-and-white print fabrics
› 58in square wadding (batting)
› 58in square backing fabric
› 15in fabric for binding

NOTE: USE ¼IN SEAM ALLOWANCE QUANTITIES BASED ON FABRIC 42IN WIDE

---

1 For the border, cut the following from the white fabric (across the length of the fabric):

› One 7½ x 28in strip
› One 19¼ x 35in strip
› One 19¼ x 46¾in strip
› One 7½ x 53¾in strip

2 To make Block C (the middle row), cut the following:

› Five 2in grey print squares (centre)
› Five 1½ x 2in white strips (strip 1)
› Five 1½ x 3in yellow print strips (strip 2)
› Five 1½ x 3in white strips (strip 3)
› Five 1½ x 4in black-and-white print strips (strip 4)
› Five 1½ x 4in yellow print strips (strip 5)
› Five 1½ x 5in white strips (strip 6)
› Five 1½ x 5in white strips (strip 7)
› Five 1½ x 6in white strips (strip 8)

3 Take a grey square and strip 1. Sew them together using ¼in seam allowance and press the seams away from the centre square. Then sew strip 2 on an adjacent side and press as before. Continue to add the remaining strips in this way, turning the centre by 90 degrees each time you join another strip. The finished block should measure 6in square.

4 Repeat step 3 another time to make a total of five Block C.

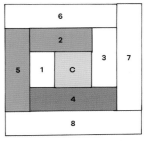

Block C

The limited colour palette has helped to give this quilt a minimalist feel, but an equally interesting result could be achieved by reversing the fabrics, with the Log Cabin blocks made from pale, plain fabrics and the border from a darker, patterned fabric.

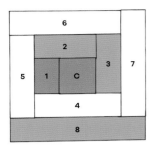

Block B

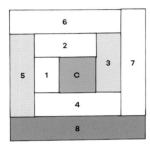

Block A

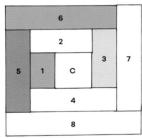

Block D

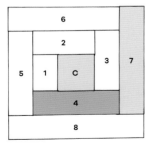

Block E

5 To make Block B (the second row), cut the following:

› **Five 2in black-and-white print squares (centre)**

› **Five 1½ x 2in black-and-white print strips (strip 1)**

› **Five 1½ x 3in yellow print strips (strip 2)**

› **Five 1½ x 3in yellow print strips (strip 3)**

› **Five 1½ x 4in white strips (strip 4)**

› **Five 1½ x 4in white strips (strip 5)**

› **Five 1½ x 5in white strips (strip 6)**

› **Five 1½ x 5in white strips (strip 7)**

› **Five 1½ x 6in yellow print strips (strip 8)**

6 Following the same method as in steps 2 and 3, sew the strips together to make five Block B.

7 To make Block A (half used in the top row and half used in the bottom row), cut the following:

› **Five 2in yellow print squares (centre)**

› **Five 1½ x 2in white strips (strip 1)**

› **Five 1½ x 3in white strips (strip 2)**

› **Five 1½ x 3in grey print strips (strip 3)**

› **Five 1½ x 4in white strips (strip 4)**

› **Five 1½ x 4in grey print strips (strip 5)**

› **Five 1½ x 5in white strips (strip 6)**

› **Five 1½ x 5in white strips (strip 7)**

› **Five 1½ x 6in black-and-white print strips (strip 8)**

8 Following the same method as in steps 2 and 3, sew the strips together to make five Block A.

9 To make Block D (the fourth row), cut the following:

› **Five 2in white squares (centre)**

› **Five 1½ x 2in yellow print strips (strip 1)**

› **Five 1½ x 3in white strips (strip 2)**

› **Five 1½ x 3in grey print strips (strip 3)**

› **Five 1½ x 4in white strips (strip 4)**

› **Five 1½ x 4in black-and-white print strips (strip 5)**

› **Five 1½ x 5in yellow print strips (strip 6)**

› **Five 1½ x 5in white strips (strip 7)**

› **Five 1½ x 6in white strips (strip 8)**

10 Following the same method as in steps 2 and 3, sew the strips together to make five Block D.

DESIGN DECISIONS

Often my quilts start with a colour palette that spontaneously comes together. The greys and yellows in this quilt were unintentionally collected and collated over two years, from places such as Liberty of London, the Festival of Quilts, and so on. There they sat in my work box until one day I put a few of them alongside each other and liked how they worked together. The prints are all quite geometric, even the trees are linear, and grey always works well with yellows such as mustard. The quilt instructions only divide up the fabrics into plain white, grey print, black-and-white print and yellow print, but the effect is made by mixing and matching the blocks. Look out for stray pre-cut 10in squares, 2½in wide strips or scrap packs to give you a wide range of fabric. If you buy fat quarters and have fabric leftovers, then a scrappy binding would look good and be in the same spirit as the pieced panel.

The way in which this quilt has been planned, with the five identical blocks, means it would lend itself well to improv-style piecing. Just make sure all the blocks are trimmed to the same size before joining into rows.

11 To make Block E (half used in the top row and half used in the bottom row), cut the following:

› **Five 2in grey print squares (centre)**

› **Five 1½ x 2in white strips (strip 1)**

› **Five 1½ x 3in white strips (strip 2)**

› **Five 1½ x 3in white strips (strip 3)**

› **Five 1½ x 4in yellow print strips (strip 4)**

› **Five 1½ x 4in white strips (strip 5)**

› **Five 1½ x 5in white strips (strip 6)**

› **Five 1½ x 5in grey print strips (strip 7)**

› **Five 1½ x 6in white strips (strip 8)**

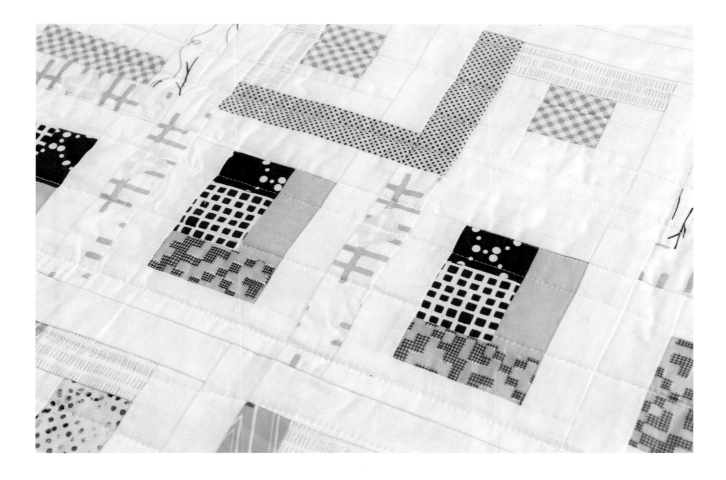

12 Following the same method as in steps 2 and 3, sew the strips together to make five Block E.

13 Using the project photograph of the finished quilt for guidance, lay out the blocks into rows:

› **The C blocks in the middle row all face the same way**

› **The B blocks in the second row and the D blocks in the fourth row are randomly rotated**

› **The A and E blocks in the top and bottom rows have been mixed and placed to face different ways.**

You can follow my layout or place your blocks as you wish. Sew the blocks together into rows, press, then sew the rows together. The panel should measure 28in square.

14 Sew the border strips to the quilt in the following order:

› 7½ x 28in strip to the left-hand side

› 19¼ x 35in strip to the bottom

› 19¼ x 46¾in strip to the right-hand side

› 7½ x 53¾in strip to the top

15 Press the quilt top. Layer the backing, wadding (batting) and quilt top, then quilt as desired (refer to Finishing: Layering a Quilt and Quilting).

16 Bind the quilt. I wanted the binding to fade into the background so I used a pale grey fabric and the single-fold binding method with mitred corners (refer to Finishing: Binding). I cut six strips 1¼in wide across the width of the fabric then joined them together end to end.

▲ *I machine quilted random wavy lines across the quilt using a white thread.*

OPTICAL EFFECTS

Here we explore designs that play with our perception. This style creates captivating and sometimes unsettling work as the eye struggles to bridge the gap between how something is and how it looks. Traditional quilt makers will be familiar with the 3D effect of Attic Window, or Storm at Sea, which looks from afar as if created by curved piecing. In modern quilt making, with less emphasis on regular grids and symmetrical designs, there is wide scope for visual trickery to provoke the viewer's curiosity.

▼ *Caroline Hadley's Sound Maze quilt (**Modern Patchwork** magazine) is a wonderfully bold example of two colours used in a repetitive design for an optical effect, and your eye starts to run along the lines to see where the pattern ends. The large-scale, regular-sized sections mean that it is not too unsettling, so it would look equally at home on the wall in a modern interior or on a bed.*

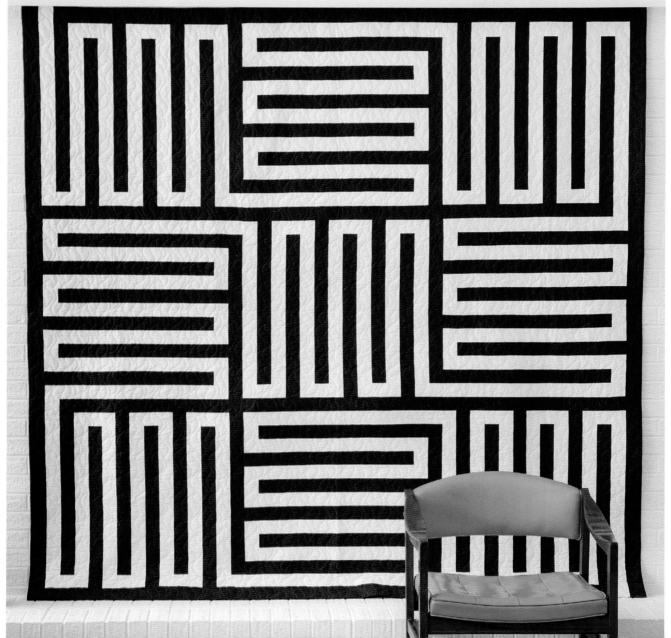

PHOTO CREDIT Matt Graves

▲ *A huge amount of energy exudes from Janae Bissinger's Streamers quilt (**McCall's Quilting**). In theory, a small number of different fabrics used to make identical blocks should create a fairly calm effect, but the high contrast and sharp angular piecing means the eye is taken on a journey, finding it difficult to settle as it follows the lines. This quilt has been constructed using clever fast strip piecing techniques and plain cotton fabrics, visually, it is dazzling, a real show stopper.*

A
Tumbling Blocks

B
Tumbling Blocks variation

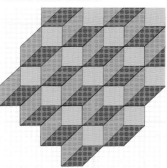

THE 3D ILLUSION

When pattern and colour are carefully planned, it can be straightforward to achieve a 3D effect in a quilt if the principles of light falling on an object (i.e., shaded at the back) are applied. Tints, tones and shades can be used to get the desired results. An easy way to understand this is to look at the traditional Tumbling Blocks layout. This consists of a repeated diamond patch (A), which looks three-dimensional when light, medium and dark colours are used; usually English paper pieced, it can be easily machine sewn if each diamond is divided into two triangles (this means you don't have to deal with inset seams). The Tumbling Blocks principle can be applied to other shapes (B).

PHOTO CREDIT: Matt Graves

▲ *The colours in the Fancy Transparencies quilt designed by Rebecca Severt (**Modern Patchwork** magazine) have been cleverly chosen to create a look of transparency – as if layers of coloured acetate have been placed on top of each other. As the three colours in each block graduate from dark to light it gives the impression of the dark centres receding into the background – or are they popping out from the front? The variety of low-volume background fabrics adds to the feeling of movement, although the overall effect is very calming.*

TRANSPARENCY

Transparent fabrics, such as organza, can be used to make a piece of patchwork that can be hung up at a window, but the optical effect of transparency can be created from opaque (non-transparent) fabrics by the clever use of colour. Familiarise yourself with the colour wheel (see the Colour chapter) and what to expect when one colour is placed on top of another. For example, overlap red and yellow transparent fabrics, then orange is the colour made, so to create a transparent effect when working with red and yellow opaque fabrics, an orange fabric needs to sit between them. You can also play with light and dark fabric in the same way (A, B).

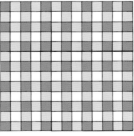

A

To create the gingham quilt design, light and dark fabrics have been chosen to represent the dark squares where the threads in the weave cross.

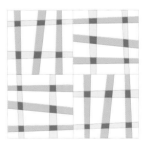

B

The torn tape quilt design takes this idea even further and the sections where the fabrics 'cross' one another take on the colour that would be seen if they were transparent pieces of paper.

*◄ The graphic Iberian Tile quilt (**Modern Patchwork** magazine) was inspired by a floor in a Spanish church. The designer, Catherine Redford, has broken it down into squares and rectangles to create an intriguing woven design. The colours are exciting and well balanced, and the symmetrical layout means the eye is not distracted from working out where the strips continue and end.*

STRIPS AND STRIPES

Simple lines of colour have such a powerful effect on our vision that interior designers will often advise to place vertical striped wallpaper in a room to make the ceiling look higher or horizontal striped wallpaper to make the room appear bigger. In quilt design, lines of colour put together in different layouts can create optical effects; the eye tries to follow the pattern and make sense of it, and interrupting the pattern can play tricks on the senses. Lines of colour can be made by using a stripe fabric, or by piecing strips together (this gives you control over strip colour and width but does take more time to prepare). Lines of quilting can also add to these effects. For inspiration, look at the work of the artist Bridget Riley.

A weaving effect can be created by designing a quilt with strips that appear to go under and over each other, as happens when cloth is woven. The resulting interlocking designs can be intriguing to look at as it is difficult to see where the lines start and finish.

PIXELLATION

Pixels are the squares or dots of colour that make up images on a computer or TV screen. When you look at a screen you cannot see them as the thousands of individual colours blended together; reduce the resolution (number of pixels) in an image, however, and they start to become visible. Pixellated quilts are usually pieced using squares – or rectangles and triangles – but can also be made from other shapes, such as appliqué circles (see pointillism for inspiration). When put together, they create an image that looks particularly effective from afar (the effect of a curve can be achieved without working with curved pieces, for example), but close-up the viewer loses the overall design and simply sees the fabric pieces. They can look complex, but if you think in terms of each colour being represented by a square, as in a cross-stitch pattern, it simplifies things.

If using a basic shape such as a square, pixellated quilts are fairly easy to sew together, but they take quite a bit of planning to get the fabrics in the correct place. For a simple way of pixellating an image see the Pixellation Exercise, but if you want to work on something more complex, with different colours and motifs, then you may need to enlarge your image to poster size to get the detail you require; for this, large sheets of tracing paper are available from art shops. You can either colour in your design as you go, choosing your fabrics first and shading to match them, or buy fabric to correspond with your pen colours later.

Cross stitchers may be familiar with software and apps that can be used to transfer an image to a paper design of squares with a colour reference. For quilters, a similar online service is offered by youpatch.com, who, for a fee, will turn an uploaded image into a working guide, as well as advise on fabric quantities and how to sew the design together in sections.

Playing with stripes exercise

This exercise explores how stripes can be used in quilt design. You'll need three 8in square pieces of striped paper, two with horizontal stripes and one with stripes running at a 45-degree angle. You can try this exercise on your computer by following your software instructions and saving the different versions as you go.

1 From one piece of paper cut sixteen 2in squares. The quickest way to do this is to use your rotary cutter and ruler, but as paper will blunt the blade, do use an old blade. (Alternatively, draw the grid on the back of the paper and cut using paper scissors.) Lay out the squares in a four by four grid with the stripes facing the same way (A).

2 Now rotate every other block the opposite way to give a woven effect (B). Then randomly rotate a few more squares (C).

3 Take the piece of paper with the stripes running at a 45-degree angle and cut it into eight 2in squares. Use these squares to replace some of the squares in your design to make different designs (D, E, F).

4 Now cut a circle out of the middle of a piece of striped paper. Place the circle back into the aperture and spin it around so that its stripes are at a different angle (G), then glue the striped paper sheet to a piece of backing paper (this does not have to be striped!). Make four copies of this design in all. Place them in a two by two grid, alternating the direction of the stripes (H). Compare how one looks to the impact of four together.

To take things further, try changing the colours or the spacing of the stripes or cut the striped paper into different shapes, such as triangles and diamonds, with the lines running different ways to see what designs appear.

A

B

C

D

E

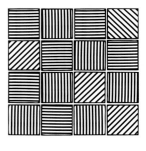

F

G

H

◄ *The Pixelated wall quilt (Karen Ackva, **Quiltmaker** magazine) has a strong visual presence. Initially, this looks to be the result of the vivid colour palette, with bright colours, including the primaries blue, red and yellow, having a strong contrast with the paler background. As you look closer you see other design concepts such as the changing scale and the diagonal positioning of the strips which gives them the dynamic feel of a flash, as if they are just passing through. Seen up close, the design looks abstract, and it is not until you stand further back that the areas that give a feeling of depth and make it look as if the strips are breaking down come into view.*

Pixellation exercise

This exercise describes how to achieve a simple pixellated design from a photograph by changing it into a grid of coloured squares, which can be used to plan a quilt. Using only a few colours, it is designed as an introduction to the technique.

1 Print out your photo (a slightly blurred image often works best). The example used was A4 (US letter) size, but for more detail you may want to print it larger. Draw or print out a grid on a same size sheet of tracing paper. Each square will represent a piece of fabric, so consider the scale.

2 Place the photo on your work surface and tape the corners to hold it in place, then tape the tracing paper grid on top (A). Working your way around the edge, colour in each square that forms part of the outline, and when you have finished, shade the inner parts (B).

3 To get a clearer guide, you can redraw the image onto graph paper (C).

4 Tape your graph paper guide onto a wall and stand back to view it. Does it look as you want it to? If so, then decide how large you want your finished piece to be. For example, if a design is 36 squares across and each square represents 1in, then the finished piece will be 36in square.

A

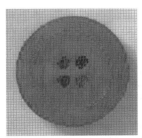

B

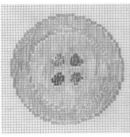

C

Project 7:
MONOCHROME HOOP PICTURE

This project is a subtle play on an optical effect. When I showed it to friends, they disagreed about whether I had used just one stripe fabric or two, as some areas look black and white and others grey and white. In fact, it is all the same fabric, illustrating how the different directions of the lines alter how it is perceived. When sewing your pieces together, don't worry about lining the stripes up perfectly as it is the little interruptions to the line that move the eye along.

Finished size

10in diameter

You will need

› One fat quarter of narrow stripe fabric

› 15in square backing fabric

› 10in diameter embroidery hoop

› 25in length of ¾in wide ribbon

1 Using the templates (see Templates) prepare the patches using the English paper piecing method (refer to Quilt Basics: Piecing). Make sure the stripes are following the direction described (A), lining up the paper shape along a line so they are consistent:

› Two hexagons with horizontal stripes

› Two diamonds with horizontal stripes

› Two diamonds with vertical stripes

› Six kites with diagonal stripes

› Four kites with horizontal stripes

› Two half hexagons with stripes facing left

› Two half hexagons with stripes facing right

2 Following the finished project photograph as a guide for layout, place the fabric pieces on your work surface. Starting with the middle section (B), sew the fabric pieces together using whip or ladder stitch. Work your way from the inner patches to the outer ones until all are joined.

3 Cut the backing fabric into a circle with a diameter of approximately 14½in using pinking shears if you have them. Pin then tack (baste) the pieced panel onto the backing fabric and stitch in place: I used small slip stitches and went around the white areas using white thread, then the black areas using black thread.

4 Make a small incision on the back of the work through the backing fabric only. Remove tacking (basting) stitches (if used), then carefully place a finger between the layers and remove all the papers.

5 Give the pieced panel a press, then secure it centrally in the hoop.

6 Sew a circle of long running stitches in the middle of the excess fabric (between hoop and raw edge). Gently pull on the running stitch threads to gather the fabric, then tie to secure. Loop the ribbon through the space under the screw, adjust the length to suit, and hang to display.

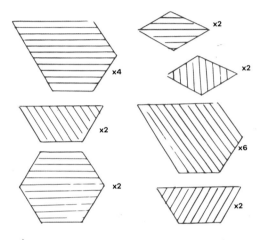

A
Fabric patches required

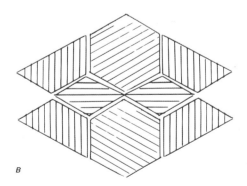

B

PLAYING WITH SHAPES

The graphic appeal of shapes means they are a strong visual theme in modern quilts. They can be used in many ways, from just two or three shapes making up a minimalist design, to lots of shapes repeated for a highly patterned design. When drafting ideas for a modern pieced or appliquéd quilt, taking the layout down to just the basic shapes and exploring how they interact can be a good starting place.

▲ *Kevin Kosbab's Retro Ring placemat (**50 Fat Quarter Makes**) shows how the simple positioning of two organic outline shapes can create an interesting and balanced design. The quilting stops before the appliqué shapes, which means they stand out from the background.*

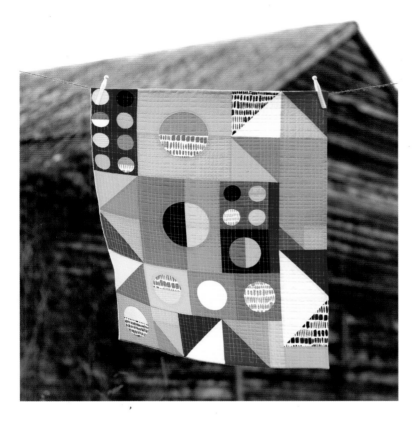

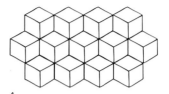

◀ *The different shapes in deep, bright colours on the Bricks and Fences quilt by quilter and printmaker Lucie Summers (**Quilt Improv**) makes it look almost like a collage. The similarity in the form of the shapes means that, despite the differences in size and colour, they work cohesively together, giving the finished piece a look similar to an abstract painting.*

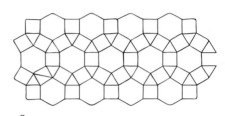

A

B

GEOMETRIC SHAPES

These are the building blocks in traditional quilts, with many patchwork piecing techniques derived from geometric shapes, such as triangles, squares and circles. The preciseness of these forms means they are irresistible to use in quilt design, particularly if your pattern is very graphic, resulting in clean lines that can look visually striking. They can be used on their own or next to each other, spaced with a strip in between or layered on top of one another. Simple designs are easy to draft and plan using computer software or graph paper, and they can be a good basis for exploring interesting colour layouts.

When working with a shape to design a quilt, think carefully about what you call it. For example, if using circles in green fabrics, you might be tempted to name it Green Circles, but Emerald Spheres is a much more interesting name and, as spheres are three-dimensional, this could lead you to explore placing the circles on a dark border to make them look as if they are bouncing out from the quilt.

TESSELLATION

Patterns made from geometric shapes that can be placed together without leaving any gaps are called tessellations, and this can be achieved using just one shape or a combination of shapes (A, B). These designs can be sewn by hand or on a machine using the Y-seam method if three patches join at the same point. To explore tessellated quilt design, cut out some shapes such as hexagons or pentagons and lay them out to see what you come up with, then try cutting the shapes up into sections and have another go.

ORGANIC SHAPES

With their perfect form, geometric shapes rarely appear in nature, so organic shapes (such as hand-cut circles) can look appealing to the eye, particularly when using work that has a more spontaneous approach, such as improv or some appliqué methods. While drawing geometric shapes requires precision, organic shapes can be produced in a much freer way, by drawing with a wide paintbrush, for example, or roughly cutting out paper with scissors. For inspiration with organic shapes, take a look at the cut-out work of the artist Henri Matisse – the variation in scale, differences in motifs, and the process taken to develop the work is fascinating.

ABSTRACT DESIGN

Abstract designs are commonly seen in modern quilting with these quilts employing the principles of shape, line and colour to result in a piece intended to be viewed on a wall. If new to designing abstractly, a good starting point is a figurative image. Imagine, for example, a table set for breakfast. The view from the side gives a clear view of the items – a bowl, a pot of jam perhaps – and the eye can easily identify them. However, viewed from above, you see just shapes – the eye does not recognise the objects and the composition is broken down into shape, colour and line, and how the elements interact. You can also abstract a figurative image by cropping in on a small area of it. If you are interested in developing abstract quilts, research how different artists have worked within the genre. I'd recommend the Cubist work of artists such as Juan Gris and the Expressionist work of artists such as Wassily Kandinsky.

Paper shapes exercise

This exercise explores the design potential of a single shape and how it can be developed to create abstract designs. My designs based on triangles are shown for reference but do develop your own. Don't spend too much time on each as the more you make, the more likely you will be to find something that excites you, and that makes you want to explore ways of developing the composition in fabric.

1 You will need two pieces of paper in different colours – I used A2 size sheets and painted them using liquid watercolour, although you could use magazine pages or printed papers. Choose your shape – for my samples I chose a triangle that was 1½ x 3in. Cut about six triangles to give you shapes to start, then cut more as you go.

2 Develop four designs that use the triangle shapes on a background. They can be positioned any way you wish, experiment with placing them in different ways (A).

3 Next, draft another four designs, but this time cut up the triangles and place them slightly apart with the background colour showing through (B).

4 Finally, mix the background and triangle colours to create some designs that use counterchange (where a colour and/or shape is reversed). Start to layer shapes on top of each other (C).

The designs in steps 3 and 4 start to explore the idea of negative space – repeat them using more than one shape and different colours to see what other designs develop.

A

B

C

Abstract quilt design exercise

This exercise is aimed at collating ideas for making a mini quilt (or scale up or repeat to make a full-size quilt). I use paper, pencils and marker pens to draft my designs, but it can also be done with paint. Start by drawing squares onto your background paper (mine were 7in but they can be whatever size you wish). I have added information about how I would stitch the sample designs but use your own skills and preference to think about how you would assemble yours.

Version 1

1 Draw two random lines across the square, then draw two circles on top (cups and glasses are ideal to draw around) (A).

2 Colour in the different areas. You can choose to have the circles the same colour or to divide them up where the line intersects (B) (you could also explore transparency here – see Optical Effects). If making up, I would piece the background, then appliqué the circles using the raw-edge appliqué method (see Appliqué: Raw-Edge Appliqué).

Version 2

1 Draw two large shapes, then on top draw some strips across them. Consider how the strips overlap the shapes and how far apart they are spaced (C).

2 Colour in the different areas (D). If making up, I would piece the background in sections using foundation piecing, then add the strips on top using the bias strip appliqué method (see Appliqué: Other Appliqué Methods).

Version 3

1 Draw a rectangle, then draw another one behind it. Rub out the lines where they overlap – it should now look like one rectangle is in front of the other. Continue drawing rectangles in this way to develop a layered effect (E).

2 Colour in the design (F). If making up, I would draft a grid to use as a guide for piecing, and sew it with squares and rectangles.

Version 4

1 Take a photograph of a building. Select one area, then enlarge on a photocopier. Select the main lines in the image and trace them (G).

2 Colour in the areas (H). If making up, I would use templates to machine piece the design.

Try this exercise with collage, move elements around to position them where you want them before gluing them down.

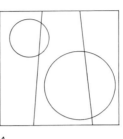

A

B

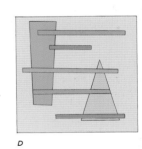

C

D

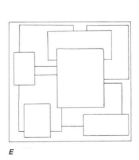

E

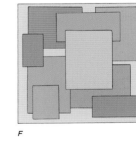

F

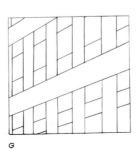

G

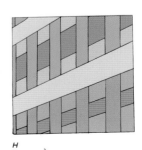

H

DESIGN DECISIONS

This quilt top was made in an improv-led way, starting with randomly cut squares and rectangles which were placed on a design wall, to which other pieces were matched, sewn and trimmed down if needed: option 1 in the instructions. I have added option 2, based on a grid drafted after the quilt was finished, for you to loosely use as a guide if you prefer, but follow your own instincts for shape and colour. For example, you could make some of the seams at a slant to follow the angle of the shapes, or piece some of the patches before joining. The pattern allows for extra fabric so you have enough to play around with.

Project 8:
RELEASE THE SHAPES QUILT

Sometimes I love a fabric so much I am hesitant to use it. This print fabric, designed by Yumi Yoshimito, had been sitting on my shelf for a few years and I wanted to use it in a special way. I had an idea for a quilt with a patched background and shapes appliquéd on top and this fabric seemed ideal. I matched it with some of Leslie Morgan's hand-dyed cotton sateen and the colours started to pop, especially the contrast between the print and the plain.

Finished size

40½ x 41½in

You will need

› 20in x WOF printed fabric
› 15in x WOF each of five different plain fabrics
› Paper-backed fusible web
› 44 x 45in backing fabric
› 44 x 45in wadding (batting)
› 16in x WOF binding fabric

NOTE: USE ¼IN SEAM ALLOWANCE QUANTITIES BASED ON FABRIC 42IN WIDE

Making patchwork top option 1 semi-improv

1 Cut three or four pieces from your fabrics then place them on a design wall or floor. Start cutting and laying small pieces next to them. Note, you can make the pieced background whatever size you wish although if making it larger you will need to adapt the wadding and backing requirements.

2 Sew pieces together to join them into panels, then use odd shapes or strips to join the panels together, cutting additional fabric as needed (you may need to sew partial seams when you join panels together). At the end, trim the piece square if needed.

Making patchwork top option 2 cutting shapes first

1 Follow the piecing diagram to cut your fabrics (the sizes shown are finished sizes so remember to add on seam allowance).

2 Join the pieces together, working in sections and using the partial seam technique as required (see Piecing: Partial and Inset Seams).

Completing the quilt

3 Press the quilt top and prepare the shapes. I cut my shapes (see Templates) freehand and made more than I needed to give me choices about what to place and where. Refer to the sizes of your patches for guidance on how big to cut them. To cut one shape, fuse the paper-backed fusible web to the wrong side of the fabric following the manufacturer's instructions, then take a pair of scissors and cut out the shape.

4 Place the shapes on the pieced quilt top, being aware of the lines created by the background fabrics. When you are happy with the layout fuse them into position. If your quilt is to be washed then stitch around each of the shapes (refer to Quilt Basics: Appliqué).

5 Press the quilt top. Layer the backing, wadding (batting) and quilt top, then quilt as desired (refer to Finishing: Layering a Quilt and Quilting). As my quilt is not to be washed, the quilting held the shapes in place. It was long-arm quilted in a grid design worked in two layers, horizontally then vertically. After quilting I added several more shapes on top of the quilt, sewing around the edge of each one to secure them.

6 Bind the wall hanging. I used the facing method (refer to Finishing: Binding) and I cut the strips 3½in wide so that I have a wide strip on the back.

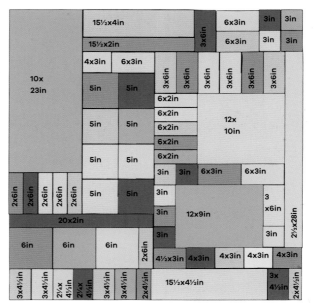

Piecing diagram for patchwork top option 2. Measurements given are width x height and are the finished size of each piece and do not include seam allowance.

MODERN TRADITIONALISM

Modern traditionalism refers to an approach to quilt design that takes inspiration from traditional quilts whilst applying some of the parameters of modern quilting, such as asymmetry or alternative grid layout. For those who learnt their skills by making traditional quilts it can be an irresistible step into modern quilting, and for those new to designing their own quilts, adding a new take on an established design can be an easy way to begin, by playing with scale or colour, for example.

▲ *Sarah J. Maxwell's Coming Unwound quilt (**Modern Patchwork magazine**) is an impressive 51in square. Considering that blocks would usually be 9in, 12in or 16in square, this design based on the traditional Spool Block is super-supersized. The large scale has been used to allow space to play with design, with the fabrics in the background cleverly planned to give an effect of transparency.*

SAMPLER QUILTS

Sampler quilts are often made as a skill builder and traditionally they sample a different patchwork design in each block – a way to learn, practise and demonstrate a variety of techniques. They can also be made using one technique, such as foundation paper piecing, or one shape, such as blocks made from triangles, or from a mix of different techniques, such as appliqué and English paper piecing. Traditionally, sampler quilts are presented in a regular grid format with sashing and/or borders. In modern sampler quilts this layout is often altered to present blocks in a new way. If you enjoy making blocks, or have some leftover from a previous project or workshop, do play around with layouts and look to see how others are using them in an alternative way.

The principles of repeats in pattern design can be interesting to apply to laying out sampler quilts and some options are explored below.

Mix of block sizes *This can look really exciting, and be made from different blocks as shown, or the same one repeated in different sizes. It can be a challenge to plan the re-sizing of blocks to fit. Start with a grid of regular dimensions (4in, 8in, 12in squares), then fill with block designs. For a very busy design, plan the colour carefully to help define the different areas.*

Square *Blocks are laid out next to each other – a versatile layout ranging from blocks sewn next to each other to plain or patterned squares placed at regular (or irregular) intervals.*

Brick *Similar to half-drop, the blocks are offset in rows. As the blocks at the end of every other row are cropped, it works best with machine pieced blocks that can be cut, or designs that can be planned so only half a block is made.*

Half-drop *With this layout, blocks are slightly offset in columns. This can work particularly well with improv blocks as it is structured, but has a feel of disorder.*

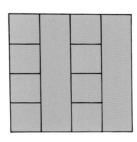

Strip *The blocks can be placed in one or more strips, either vertically or horizontally. If they go through the centre they can create a flash of eye-catching pattern, to the side they can look slightly less bold but the asymmetrical layout provokes curiosity. This design usually requires a little thought as to how the plain areas will be quilted, although do remember they could be a patterned fabric.*

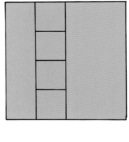

On-point *This is a traditional layout that can look really effective when combined with design theories such as negative space.*

Don't be afraid to explore traditional fabric prints for modern quilt designs. William Morris style prints, for example, used to make a quilt with an unusual block layout, can produce an exciting and unexpected piece of work.

▲ *Susan Briscoe's Ranru wall hanging (**Simple Sashiko**) features different designs made using the sashiko technique, a traditional form of stitching developed in northern Japan in which this maker is an expert. The muted shot cottons used to make the irregular background grid work well together, drawing the viewer's eye to each patch of stitching. This piece could have been worked with a regular grid, but by making it irregular it adds interest and gives it a modern feel.*

INTERRUPTING A BLOCK

One way to add a modern slant to a traditional block is by altering the typical layout. There are many ways a block can be 'interrupted', such as through stretching (A), cropping (B), or by adding strips between the patches (C). All start with a standard block that is then altered in some way.

A
Stretching a block is an interesting way to play with proportion, turning a well-known block, such as the Shoo Fly block shown here, into something unexpected.

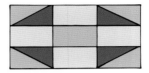

B
An example of block cropping – here the Shoo Fly block has been cut in half then joined on the width. While cropping is usually done by cutting into a finished whole block, the same effect can be pre-planned – draw the block on paper, work out what part of the block you want to use for your design, then draft the pattern from this.

NESTING A BLOCK

This is where a block is placed in the centre of another block. It works well with traditional designs that have a square of fabric in the centre, such as Sawtooth Star. The centre block can be a smaller version of the larger block, or something completely different. By using the outside of the large block as a frame, it makes an interesting effect. To explore this technique further, see Nesting a Block Exercise.

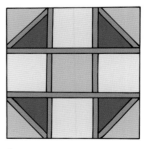

C
Adding strips between patches alters the scale and proportion of a block and can be a good way to bring together scrap fabrics. Decide on the strip widths, then adjust the block to add them in every time you sew patches together. With a nod to the sashing seen in traditional quilts, the use of a pale solid colour can give the eye room to rest.

BORDER BREAKING

Breaking the frame by taking a block into the border works in partnership with colour choice and grid layout and can be an interesting way to add detail to a traditional design (A). It can be successful using simple one-patch shapes, such as diamonds, too. The background colour will be important for this type of quilt design as the negative space will make it appear that the block or shape is moving off into another space. To design a quilt like this, draw a grid for the centre, then start to add more shapes around the edge. Finally, draw in lines to work out where the fabric pieces will be. The balance of the shapes that have moved away from the main body of the quilt will be important, so audition a few different designs before starting.

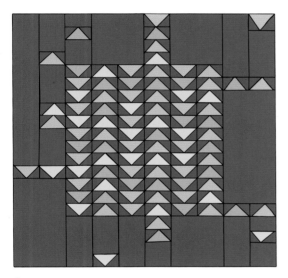

A
Units or blocks that are 'scattered' into the border can result in interesting effects. Not only do they soften a border, they also play with the design concepts of negative space and altered grids.

PLAYING WITH SCALE

Traditional blocks can be altered for modern quilt making by changing their scale to be very large or very small. Blocks that are supersized can be bold and interesting, and when hung on a wall look like a piece of art, and a quilt made this way has a minimalist feel that fits in better with modern interiors. There are a few technical issues, however: if making triangles a yardstick (metre ruler) can be helpful, and you should sew long seams slowly to make sure they are accurate. At the other end of the spectrum, working small (even miniature) scale can be challenging and there are a few things that can help, such as making sure the fabric is not too thick, using a smaller stitch length than usual, and trimming seam allowances down to ⅛in after they are sewn to reduce bulk.

▲ *The use of colour and symmetry in the Broadcast quilt by Brigit Dermott (**Modern Patchwork** magazine) gives it a 'balanced feel'. Inspired by traditional quilts, it uses two traditional patchwork units, the quarter circle (Drunkard's Path) and orange peel, at a bold larger scale to give a graphic, modern look.*

Medallion quilt exercise

It can be interesting to apply modern quilt design principles to traditional layouts. The traditional medallion (also known as frame) quilt layout is one where the patchwork designs work their way out from the centre. While a medallion design can look complex, if you start with the overall dimensions of the frames then draw the blocks into them, it is easy to plan. In this exercise, you start with a fairly traditional design to get to grips with the principle, but this can then lead off into different directions, for example an asymmetric improv design or to experiment with negative space.

1 Using the diagrams for guidance, draw, photocopy or trace one of the medallion grid designs, choosing to work with either an asymmetrical (A) or a symmetrical layout (B). For my sample layout, steps 2–4, I have used the symmetrical layout.

2 Draw a design in the centre, then colour in the first border (C).

3 Then, into the next frame (shown as squares on my layout) draw a design such as half-square triangles, or divide each one into four squares (D).

4 Continue to fill in each frame, then colour in (E).

5 Repeat the exercise to experiment with different layouts, choosing patchwork designs that appeal to you. In image (F), I have drafted an improv design placed in an asymmetric layout.

By adding a plain border between each 'round' of patchwork, the width can be altered to make the next round fit.

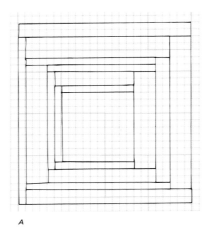

A

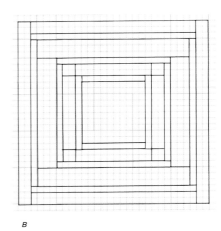

B

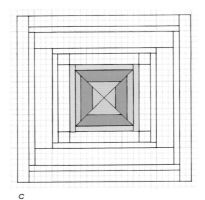

C

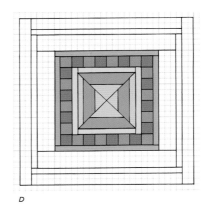

D

E

F

◄ *Katie Clark Blakesley's Sampler Quilt in Solids* (**Vintage Quilt Revival**) *is a lovely example of a quilt that is definitely modern and traditional. The structure of the quilt, with the regular grid layout and block piecing, has a traditional feel, but the use of colour and plain fabrics gives it a modern vibe.*

Nesting a block exercise

When working with traditional quilt blocks it can be interesting to see the different effects that can be created by nesting blocks in a quilt design. (It can also be a good way to make use of stray blocks in your stash by adding borders to them.) This exercise uses a star block, made using flying geese.

1 Draw a large block on graph, squared or dot grid paper (alternatively, use a computer). Make sure the design has a square in the centre (A).

2 Now draw the block again, but this time in the centre of the first one (B).

3 You could repeat once more to draw a third block, to give you three blocks nesting inside each other.

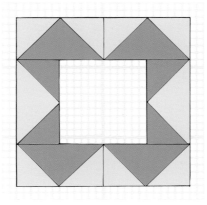

A

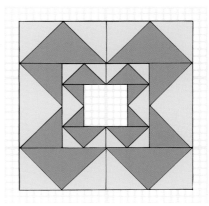

B

Project 9:
COLOUR STEPS QUILT

I have lots of odd pieces of fabric in my stash so often use them to make colour-themed blocks. I have used just four of these pieced blocks for this quick quilt, laying them out in an alternative way to a traditional block quilt. The low-volume, colour-coordinated backgrounds help the blocks to stand out, and the fabric in the centre of each block is the same as the strip, so it looks as if the stars are floating on top.

Finished size

48in square approx

You will need

› A selection of green, pink, yellow and blue fabrics for the blocks (see steps for details)
› One 20in x WOF strip of pale pink, pale yellow, pale green and pale blue fabrics for the background
› 52in square wadding (batting)
› 52in square backing fabric
› 12in x WOF binding fabric

NOTE: USE ¼IN SEAM ALLOWANCE QUANTITIES BASED ON FABRIC 42IN WIDE

The finished blocks are 12in square, so if you have been making quilts for a while you may well have some stray blocks in your stash that you could use.

1 From the four pale background fabrics cut a 12½in x WOF strip and put to one side.

2 Cut fabrics for the green block:
› Four 3⅞in squares for the flying geese backgrounds
› Four 3½in squares for the corners
› One 7¼in square for the flying geese

3 From the leftover pale green background fabric cut one 6½in square.

4 Take the 7¼in square and the four 3⅞in squares and make the side units following the instructions for making four flying geese units at a time (see Piecing: Triangles).

5 Lay out all the green pieces of fabric to make the Star block. Sew them into rows (A), then sew the rows together (B). This completes one block.

6 Following steps 2–5, make the pink, yellow and blue blocks.

7 From the 12½in x WOF strips of background fabric set aside in step 1 cut:
› One 36½ x 12½in strip from the pale green and pale blue fabrics
› One 12½in square and one 24½ x 12½in strip from the pale pink and pale yellow fabrics

8 Sew the blocks and strips into rows, then sew the rows together.

9 Press the quilt top. Layer the backing, wadding (batting) and quilt top, then quilt as desired (refer to Finishing: Layering a Quilt and Quilting); mine was long-arm quilted with a different design in each strip, which was influenced by the shapes in the print fabrics used for the blocks.

10 Bind the quilt. I cut 2¼in wide strips and used the double-fold binding method with mitred corners (refer to Finishing: Binding).

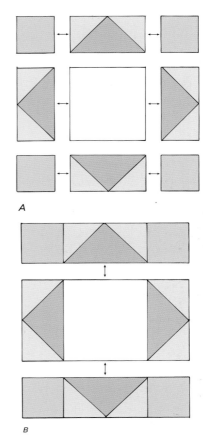

A

B

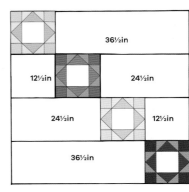

C

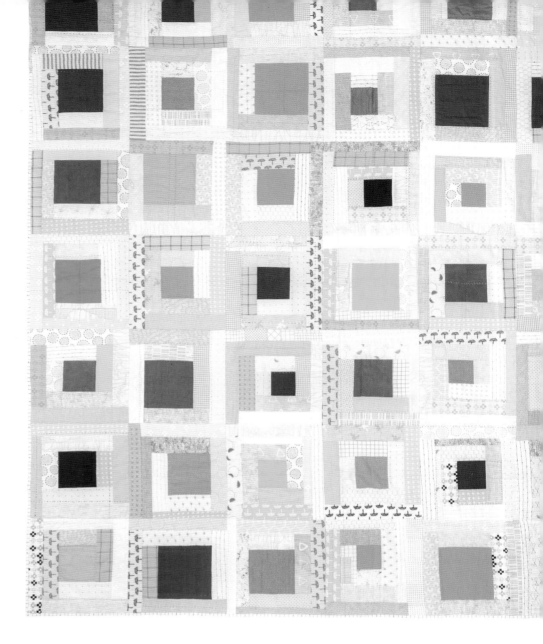

MAKING YOUR WAY

For many quilters, modern quilting is about more than just making quilts, it is about finding self-expression and fulfillment through working with cloth, fitting the sewing process into a present-day lifestyle and being part of a supportive community. This chapter covers these themes, with information, advice and hopefully some inspiration for mapping out your own unique quilt path.

▲ *Karen Lewis is a screen printer, fabric designer, quilter, and tutor based in the UK. Her patchwork projects often combine plains with fabrics that she has designed and printed, with colours carefully chosen to contrast and balance. This quilt, called Breaking Rules, is from her book* **Wabi-Sabi Sewing**, *which is based on a Japanese aesthetic ethos that focuses on the imperfect in a positive way. Although inspired by traditional quilt design, it has been interpreted in a relaxed way and shows an approach to modern quilting that is not just about design, but also an attitude to creating and making.*

USING A SKETCHBOOK

When developing quilt ideas, a sketchbook (or notebook) is a really good tool to have to hand. The type of book you use is down to personal preference: if you use paint then you may prefer a cartridge-style sketchbook from an art shop, but if pen and pencil are more your thing then you might choose a dot grid pad. Keep a well-stocked pencil case close by that includes a glue stick. If you are new to using a sketchbook the most important thing to remember is that it is personal to you. Do not be put off by a bad drawing or an idea that didn't work out – it is not being marked! To help fill those intimidating blank pages at the beginning of your sketchbook, try a daily challenge – these could be based on some of the exercises in this book, or something else entirely, such as creating a five-minute abstract collage using an old magazine. Things to put in your sketchbook could include:

› Ticket stubs – these can also act like diary entries

› Cuttings – from magazines, catalogues and newspapers

› Drawings – figurative images as well as abstract

› Mark-making – rubbings from textures

› Printing – with items found around the home

› Text – single words or a quick explanation of an idea

› Swatches – pieces of fabric or paper you like

If you design using software, then get into a habit of working on the computer and saving your pieces by date. Print out the ones you particularly like to store in your sketchbook.

RECORDING IDEAS AND INSPIRATION

Quilt inspiration can occur at any time, from spotting a newly ploughed field on the bus ride to work to noticing a design printed on the side of a mid-century saucepan at a friend's house, and that's when your phone camera is invaluable as a quick and easy way to store a visual reference. Do try to find time to delete images not required, and to edit, file or tag those remaining to ensure they are easy to find. At a quilt show, make your first photo the poster of the event, and if taking a snap of an exhibited quilt, remember to photograph the label so you know who made and designed it.

When looking for inspiration online, bookmark sites to return to later, or register to use Pinterest, an online pinboard that enables you to find, save and share images under general categories ('favourite fabrics') or specific headings ('quilt inspiration from architecture'). Remember, your boards can be seen by others unless you choose to mark them as private.

PHOTO CREDIT: Emma Kennedy

If you enjoy using social media, then most platforms have the ability to come back to ideas, for example, Twitter has the like button and Instagram has the save function.

A popular way of storing quilt ideas on paper is to use a cuttings box or folder, a place to keep patterns ripped from magazines, postcards, paint manufacturer's brochures, or exhibition catalogues.

Remember to revisit your stored inspirations often, particularly when starting a quilt project. As well as logging future ideas, don't forget to record the making of each quilt, keeping a note of such things as:

› **Project title/quilt name**

› **Design ideas**

› **Date started**

› **Date completed**

› **Fabrics used**

› **Wadding (batting) used**

› **Threads used**

› **Finished size**

▲ *Ideas and inspiration are everywhere, and I sometimes find it can be a little overwhelming. In recent years I have narrowed my work down to themes on locality, but there is also a lot of variety to be had from this. As well as spending time on a body of work based on architecture, every summer I revisit and add to sketchbooks based on the South Downs, a beautiful green hilly landscape around where I live. It connects my love of nature and being outdoors with the enjoyment of creativity and working in stitch.*

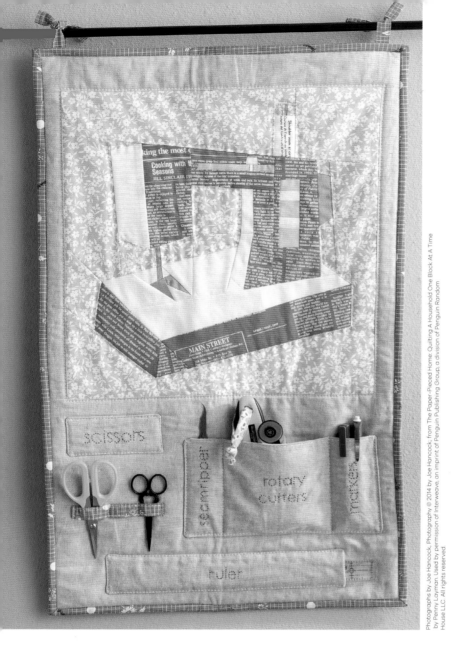

▲ *This project is a great example of what can happen when a quilter masters a specific technique, then applies their own creativity to it. Penny Layman is an expert in foundation paper piecing, and she designs fun and quirky patterns that have a retro feel. Her book,* **The Paper-Pieced Home**, *features patterns for lots of blocks, but also shows how the little pictures can be used to make a finished item.*

Quilting should be an enjoyable outlet for of self-expression. Focus on your own journey, and try not to compare yourself to others. If you find yourself being hypercritical of your work, take a step back; imperfection is what makes us human.

WORKING TO A THEME

Some find that this approach can help them to develop a body of work that shows a progression of ideas, while others find it stifling to have set boundaries. Whatever your personal take, you may discover common links in your work, be it colour, technique or subject matter. You could set yourself the challenge of choosing a specific word as the inspiration to make a mini quilt every fortnight to explore quilt making as a form of self-expression.

QUILTING COMMUNITIES

Working and socialising with other quilters has huge benefits, from sharing ideas to receiving advice. To meet other quilters in person, look out for groups who get together in settings such as libraries and village halls who might host sewing days, classes and speakers. If you can't find a group near you, chat with your local community setting as they may support you in establishing one.

Online communities are easy to find, although with so much choice it is often best to get a recommendation to locate like-minded quilters across the world. The most popular social media channels are Facebook, where there are open or closed (requiring a request to join) groups; Twitter, where you can share news and have conversations; and Instagram, a visual platform for sharing photos and updates of work, where comments and messages can be left. If you like a particular way of working, such as foundation paper piecing, look for hashtags to see posts with that tag. Facebook and Instagram users also host challenges, where someone invites others to post on a particular theme on specific days, and quilt-a-longs where a group of people work on the same project. If using social media, do follow the service providers rules to keep yourself safe.

If you enjoy sharing your work then being a member of a group often gives the opportunity to exhibit your quilts. You can find out about these opportunities online or, if you are a member of an organisation such as The Modern Quilt Guild or The Quilters' Guild of the British Isles, then newsletters can let you know about shows accepting submissions online. Some shows charge a fee for entrants, and some only accept juried in work (where a selected panel decide which quilts will be on display). Read entry forms thoroughly as there may be specific requirements, such as maximum size or labelling. There are two types of shows: those that are a display of work and those that are judged where winners receive prizes. Some shows also allow you the opportunity to sell your work.

*These Improv Pillows in Black and White (**Modern Patchwork** magazine) show how one technique and colour concept can be used to create a series of different, but co-ordinating looks. The addition of the jewel-like colours positioned across the piecing makes them intriguing to look at and softens the strong contrast between the black and white. The maker is Malka Dubrawsky, a writer, tutor and designer well known for her adroit use of colour when using cloth as a medium. As well as writing books, she has designed ranges for fabric manufacturers and dyes her own fabric which gives her work a strong distinctive style.*

MAKING A LIVING

Many quilters successfully turn their hobby into a business either by teaching or by working to commission, which might include writing patterns for magazines, designing fabric ranges, or selling finished patterns or quilts through websites such as Etsy. If you are interested in following this path, research what steps others took to get there – you might wish to undertake more formal training or seek advice on setting up a small business.

TEACHING

Whether you want to share your quilt-making skills with a group of friends informally or to be paid to teach a class at a shop, here are some tips for success:

› Communicate what the session involves and what will be achieved.

› Keep a register so you know who to expect so you can start the session promptly.

› Start with a talk on safety and set some ground rules – use of rotary cutters, no drinks near machines, etc.

› Plan the class – work out how long each part will take and what you will need to demonstrate.

› Take a break – even if it's a short class it refreshes everyone's concentration and gets people talking to one another.

› Bring everyone together at the end to share their makes and ensure all questions are answered; give students handouts to take away.

SELLING QUILTS

Pricing a quilt can be a difficult task as the cost of materials and time required can make them expensive items, but if it is your livelihood, it is important to set your charges taking into account all your outgoings, as follows:

› Materials: fabric (quilt top, backing and binding), wadding (batting), threads, other embellishments.

› Overheads: electricity (sewing machine, iron, lighting, heating); maintenance (for the pot that covers sewing machine service, replacement rotary cutter blade, etc.); professional fees (business bank account, tax advisor, studio rent, etc.); marketing costs (Etsy website, cost of a stall at an event, etc.).

› Time (multiplied by your hourly rate): as well as cutting out, quilt top assembly, layering, quilting and binding, don't forget design and researching/buying materials, and add on a percentage to cover time you are not working, such as holidays.

› Miscellaneous: courses, books and learning – remember, your experience has a value to it.

› If your quilt prices are coming out higher than you would like, consider if there are ways you can bring your costs down, such as bulk buying wadding (batting) and thread, batch making, or simplifying piecing.

› If making quilts for children, do check your local trading rules first as there may be safety guidelines you must follow.

SELLING PATTERNS

If you design your own quilts then others may pay for printed or downloadable instructions to make them. Here's a few things to consider:

› Patterns can be sold at shows, or online through your own website or selling sites such as Etsy. Once you have some experience, you could also look at wholesaling printed patterns to shops or distributors.

› Make sure your patterns are written in a consistent way and when you have finished, ask a fellow quilter to check through, or hire a technical editor.

› Using the pricing guidelines for selling quilts, work out your costs to ensure you are making a profit for your time, materials and other outgoings.

› If you want to write for magazines or books, research which publications are a good match for your style, then send a short introductory email. Give a little information about yourself and a link to a website, blog or social media (if you use them), and ask if they are accepting submissions.

You will need to comply with commercial legislation (insurance, risk assessments, accounting, data policies, etc.) and if in doubt, seek professional business advice.

Creating a mood board exercise

Mood boards are widely used in the design world to bring together a collection of ideas and express to others how they will work together. In quilting, mood boards can be used in lots of different ways, such as developing a theme or for presenting an idea.

1 Think of a theme – mine is based on 'playful brights'. Look for an image, or a selection of images, from magazines or books. Photocopy or tear out your selected image(s), find fabric or colour swatches to complement, and roughly cut them at this stage.

2 On a piece of A3 paper, card or mountboard, build up a background layer with paint or paper (A).

3 Start placing your items on the board, editing what you have selected so that they work together to present a cohesive message (B).

4 When you are happy with the placement, glue it down. (You might also wish to add some text to reinforce key ideas, such as 'Playful Brights' in this instance.)

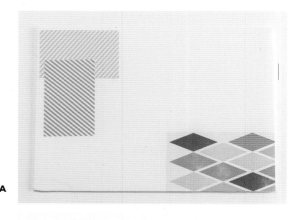

A

B

Photographing work exercise

If you are part of an online community, sharing work in progress or a finished quilt online can be immensely satisfying. Here are some ideas for styling and taking photos of your own quilts – have a go at creating each type of photo. Make sure there is good natural light and that the image is in focus, and practise cropping.

Flatlay *Place items on a surface, add accessories, then take the photo from directly above.*

Work in progress *Show the project being made and, if it is possible, include hands to add to the story being told.*

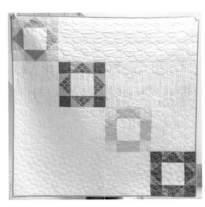

Flat shot *To get a clear view of the front, hang the quilt up, or ask a friend to hold it up for you.*

Folded/rolled *Neatly roll or fold the quilt, place it on a chair or floor, and take the photo from the side.*

Close up *Focus on a specific area you particularly like – of the quilting, piecing, or a corner of the binding.*

In use *Place your project in situ, such as on a bed, sofa or wall, to show how it will be used.*

Peek of the back *Fold over the back to show the quilting, binding and, if you have used it, a pieced backing.*

Scrunched *If you do not want to show the full finished design, scrunch the centre of the quilt.*

Out-take *This is something not usually seen, such as a view of the piecing from the back.*

DESIGN DECISIONS

Much of my work is inspired by locality, and sometimes this will be figurative or use text (for example, I have digitally printed old tickets onto fabric), with the connection not initially apparent, as for this quilt. Many of the blocks are based on streets from Victorian and Edwardian maps of roads no longer there, but where my family lived, worked or went to school. The background fabric is a loose linen weave, and this along with the minimal quilting gives the quilt a lovely soft drape.

Project 10:
ROUTES QUILT

I love working with bias appliqué strips, and the initial idea for this quilt started with sketches for a quilt with different lines and curves in each block. These began to look like road layouts to me, and at the same time I was researching old maps of my home city for a class I was teaching. So, I started playing with an idea of loosely using the shape of streets that had a personal connection to me to form the blocks, so although the end quilt has a narrative, at first glance it looks abstract.

Finished size
42 x 47¼in approx

You will need:

› 12in x WOF grey fabric for background blocks
› 24in x WOF light blue fabric for background blocks
› 24in x WOF cream fabric for background blocks
› 20 x 25in (approx) each of five fabrics in scarlet, mustard, lemon, teal and charcoal for bias strips
› 24in x WOF dark grey fabric for filler background blocks
› 46 x 52in wadding (batting)
› 46 x 52in backing fabric
› 12in x WOF binding fabric
› Pack of bias bars
› Fabric glue stick

NOTE: USE ¼IN SEAM ALLOWANCE QUANTITIES BASED ON FABRIC 42IN WIDE

1 Cut the fabrics for your background blocks. You need a total of twelve blocks. I cut nine complete squares, then pieced the other three. To make the same layout as I did, for the complete squares cut the following:

› Two 11in squares grey fabric
› Four 11in squares light blue fabric
› Three 11in squares cream fabric

2 For the pieced background squares, cut and join the pieced background blocks as follows:

› One grey 9½ x 11½in rectangle from the background block fabric, joined to one scarlet 3 x 11½in bias strip fabric (top left block)
› One cream 9½ x 11½in rectangle from the background block fabric, joined to one mustard 3 x 11½in bias strip fabric (middle right block)
› Cut and sew together one cream 5½ x 9½in rectangle and one light blue 6½ x 9½in rectangle cut from the background block fabric, then join on a charcoal 2½ x 11in bias strip fabric (second column from left at the bottom)

Trim all three pieced block squares down to measure 11in square.

3 Prepare your bias strips to the widths of the bars in your pack (refer to Appliqué: Other Appliqué Methods). My pack of bars included the following widths: ³⁄₁₆in, ¼in, ³⁄₈in and ½in. The total amount you will need depends on your appliqué design. I started by making two strips of each width from each fabric, then cut more as required.

4 Take a background square and a selection of your prepared bias strips. Place the bias strips on the background square and when you are happy with the positioning, use fabric glue to hold them in place. Be aware of the layering of the bias strips as some will go underneath others. I used old maps for reference but did not follow the lines too carefully; you may

decide to use more random layouts for your blocks. Slip stitch the bias strips in place using a toning thread each time, and if you are working with any short pieces that finish within the block, neaten by turning the end under. Complete all the bias strip appliqué blocks in this way.

5 Cut twelve 5¾ x 11in rectangles from the filler fabric. Referring to the photograph of the quilt, place the bias strip appliqué blocks in columns with a filler rectangle in between. When you are happy with the layout sew the blocks into columns, then sew the columns together.

6 Press the quilt top. Layer the backing, wadding (batting) and quilt top, then quilt as desired (refer to Finishing: Layering a Quilt and Quilting). I did not want the quilting to detract from the appliqué so I machine quilted lines about ⁵⁄₈in away from the seam line, judging it by eye and using a fine pale grey thread.

7 Bind the quilt as you desire. I used a thick shot cotton, so I stitched it using the single-fold binding method with mitred corners (refer to Finishing: Binding) with a ³⁄₈in seam allowance.

If your quilting design is minimal like mine, be sure to choose a wadding (batting) that is stable with minimal stitching.

QUILT
BASICS

SEWING BASICS

This section covers the essential skills needed when making a quilt. It opens with hand sewing, including a reference to essential stitches, then covers machine piecing, and finally templates. Getting the basics right can make it not only easier to make a quilt but streamlines the process and results in a well-made finished item.

HAND SEWING BASICS

Hand sewing is an incredibly relaxing way of stitching and is easy to pick up and put down. It can be used for piecing, appliqué and quilting, with a project made completely by hand or by mixing machine and hand methods if you prefer.

Hand Sewing Needles

When hand sewing, always use the correct needle for the job. Generally, the larger the number, the smaller the needle will be (although needle type will also affect the size) and the smaller the needle, the finer the hole made in the fabric. Hand sewing needles do blunt, and their efficiency can be affected by the natural oils transferred from your fingers, so do change your needle regularly. To prevent damage to the fabric, the needle should glide through easily without snagging. Hand sewing needles most widely used for quilt making are:

Sharps These vary in size but all have a small eye and sharp point. They are used for hand piecing, neatening thread ends when machine quilting, and stitching on binding.

Betweens/Quilting These are very small needles with a sharp point: the larger sizes can be used in a similar way to sharps, the smaller ones for traditional hand quilting.

Chenille These have a very large eye and a sharp point. They are ideal for quilting with thicker threads such as perle.

Milliner's These are long, thin needles with a sharp point. The smaller ones are good for appliqué.

Embroidery These have a long eye and a sharp point, and they are ideal for quilting with thicker threads such as perle.

Darner These are long, sharp needles and the smaller sizes are useful for tacking (basting) quilts.

Curved Some quilters like to use a curved needle for tacking (basting) quilt layers together, and the angle makes them perfect for working on 3D items.

Use thread no more than 16–18in long to prevent it from getting tangled.

MAKING A QUILTER'S KNOT

This is a fast way to make a neat knot in the end of your thread.

1 Thread the needle, then hold the end of the thread in one hand and the needle in the other and place them together to make a circle (A).

2 Place the end of the thread next to the needle and secure with your finger (B).

3 Wrap the end of the thread around the needle three times (C).

4 Keeping your finger firmly gripped over the wrapped thread, slide the needle up through your fingers (D).

5 Pull the knot down the thread (E). When you get about ¼in from the end, release your finger.

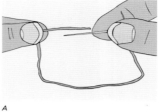

A

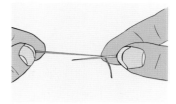

B

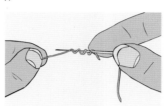

C

D

E

Hand Sewing Stitches

Here are the hand stitches most commonly used in quilt making for piecing, quilting or decorative finishes, such as embroidering quilt labels. If you are new to a stitch, practise on a piece of scrap fabric first.

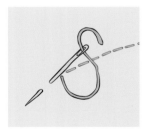

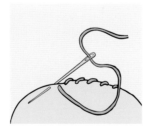

RUNNING STITCH

This forms a dashed line and it is used for sewing fabrics together as well as for embroidery. Try to make sure the stitches are an even length and adapt the size to your project. Hand quilting is a form of running stitch.

SLIP STITCH

This is used for sewing appliqué shapes to a background fabric and for finishing binding. If you require an almost invisible finish use small stitches and a thread that tones with the fabric being applied, and take the needle through to the backing fabric above where it came out and travel it along the back between stitches.

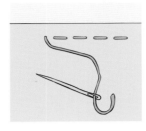

TACKING (BASTING) STITCH

This is a long form of running stitch that is designed to hold fabric layers together when sewing. It is removed at the end and, to make this easier, you may wish to start and finish this stitch without a knot.

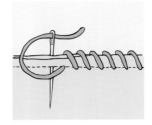

WHIP STITCH

Whip stitch, also called oversewing, is widely used in English paper piecing for joining patches together. It is also used to close turning gaps to finish a project and for sewing around raw edge appliqué (note: in this diagram the size of the stitch is exaggerated).

BACKSTITCH

This can be used instead of a running stitch when hand piecing to get an extra secure finish. It can also be used to embroider text onto quilt labels. Try to make the stitches evenly spaced – from the front, it should look like a solid line.

CROSS STITCH

This can be used for decorative embroidery as well as when hand quilting. To give a neat two-sided finish when quilting, do not take the needle to the back every time, but travel it along the middle of the quilt instead.

FRENCH KNOTS

These decorative stitches are handy for adding detail to appliqué. When making a French knot bring the needle to the front of the work and wrap the thread around it several times (the more times the larger the knot), then holding the thread taut, place the needle back through the fabric just next to where it came out. Hold the tension on the thread as the needle goes back through the fabric, then release to form the knot.

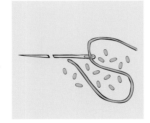

SEED STITCH

This stitch can be used decoratively for embroidery as well as to make an interesting effect when quilting. Simply take small stitches, changing the direction each time. If quilting, try to make the distance between the stitches even on the back as well as the front.

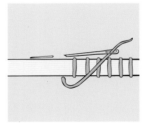

LADDER STITCH

This can be used for an invisible finish when English paper piecing or sewing on binding, and to securely close turning gaps to finish a project. The needle travels between stitches within the folded edge, working from one side of the seam to the other. You can take several stitches at a time, then gently gather them to close the seam.

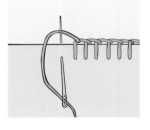

BLANKET STITCH

This stitch is ideal for sewing around appliqué, and the length and width can be adjusted to create the desired effect. The thread starts at the outside edge of the motif, then the needle is placed through the fabric on the inside edge, coming up again at the outside edge. As you pull the needle through, keep the thread behind the needle to hold it in place.

MACHINE SEWING BASICS

Speed is the main reason for the popularity of sewing machine use for making quilts. If you cut fabric carefully with a rotary cutter, then sew the pieces together with an accurate seam allowance, you will get a piece of patchwork that fits together perfectly in a short amount of time – and that is a very satisfying thing.

Sewing Machine Accessories

Any sewing machine can be used for quilt making, and if you are purchasing a new one at a shop or a show, make sure to get a demonstration so you know how to use it when you get home. With modern sewing machines, there are additional functions that can be handy, such as a needle up/down button to help when changing direction and an automatic cutter that trims threads when you have finished sewing. Add-on products include extension tables that extend the size of the machine's working area and presser feet that make it easier to sew in specific situations, such as an open-toe foot when following a line or sewing around an appliqué motif. Also, a built-in wider 'throat' area (the distance between the needle and main body of the machine) can make it easier to feed a large quilt through when quilting.

Keep a copy of your sewing machine manual close to hand (if you have mislaid it, search online as most manuals are available to download) and always use the right needle for the fabric type you are sewing. When you are not using your machine store it safely: at room temperature, out of direct sunlight, upright and covered to protect it from dust.

SEAM ALLOWANCE

In patchwork, the usual seam allowance is ¼in, and unless otherwise stated all the measurements in this book use this, so for example, for a 3in square finished a ½in will be added on for seam allowance and so it will be cut 3½in. When following your own design this needs adding on to the size of the finished patches. Occasionally seam allowance can be ⅜in or even ½in, so do read through a pattern before starting.

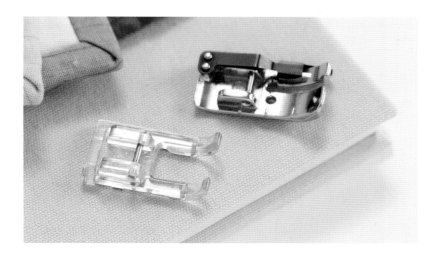

▲ A clear open-toe foot and ¼-inch foot with a guide.

THE QUARTER-INCH FOOT

When machine piecing for patchwork it is essential to get an accurate ¼in seam allowance, otherwise your patches will not fit together. A ¼-inch foot is available for most machines and is indispensable if sewing lots of patchwork as you can trust your seam allowance is accurate. Some have a guide at the edge of the foot, others use the width. You may need to adjust the needle position when using a ¼-inch foot so do refer to the manual before use. Run a test the first time you use the foot as some work best with the fabric pushed right against the edge, while others require a tiny gap (say a thread width) between the fabric and the edge of the foot.

If a ¼-inch foot is unavailable for your machine, you can make your own seam guide (see Piecing: Patchwork Basics).

Machine Sewing Needles

Often an afterthought, needle choice is important and a good-quality sewing machine needle will result in a better finish. The size of the needle will affect the hole it makes in the fabric, so use a smaller needle for finer fabric (such as voile) and a larger needle for heavier fabric (such as canvas). Most packs of needles will have two sizes on them, and the first (smaller) number is the US size and the second (larger) number is the European size. It is important to use the right needle for the job; for example, a ballpoint needle used for sewing knit fabrics when dressmaking could damage finely woven fabric when making a quilt. When piecing cotton using a 50-weight thread, a 10/70 or 12/80 needle is usually recommended; when quilting with a thicker thread, a 12/80 needle is preferred, but if working with thicker fabrics or thread, you may require a 14/90 or 16/100 needle. If in doubt, test the needle on your chosen fabrics before starting.

One of the most important things to remember when machine sewing is to change the needle regularly as they wear with repeated use, which affects the quality of the stitch. The machine needles that are most regularly used for quilt making are:

Universal A good all-purpose needle, these are a popular choice for piecing. If using a new fabric do test it first as they have a slightly rounded point.

Quilting These are sharp and are designed for sewing through layers.

Sharp (or Microtex) These are fine needles with a sharp point making them suitable for piecing and for sewing finely woven fabrics such as lawn.

Denim Sharp, strong needles for heavier weight fabrics – good for piecing cotton duck, thick linen and denim, of course, and excellent for dealing with a project that has bulk due to lots of seams.

Tips for Machine Stitching

› Before sewing, place the fabrics right sides together and press to help them hold together.

› Make sure the threads are pulled towards the back of the presser foot and start sewing from the very edge of the fabric. There is usually no need to reverse the stitching at the start and end of a line as the next seam will secure the stitching.

› Do not pull the fabric as it feeds through your machine, softly guide it and let the feed dogs pull it through. If free-motion sewing using a darning foot, gently move the fabric.

› If you need to readjust the fabric, such as when sewing around a curved appliqué shape, stop with the needle down through the fabric, lift the presser foot and rearrange as needed. When you start sewing again it will be from the exact point you stopped at.

› If your sewing needs a nudge to get started, which can happen when using bulky fabric, try using a leader. This is a piece of scrap fabric, usually at least two layers, that is sewn first, then the actual piecing is fed in after.

› When you finish sewing do not cut the top thread too short, otherwise when you start sewing again the lever can lift up and unthread the needle.

› Remove pins just before they go under the presser foot – sewing over pins can affect the timing of the machine and result in an expensive repair.

› If the fabric is distorting, try reducing the foot pressure on your sewing machine (if your machine has this function).

› If you are working on a quilt that has fabric of one colour use thread to match. If using fabrics with different colours use pale grey or beige thread as this tends to blend in.

› Thread is put onto a reel in two different ways. If it is cross wound, then it forms a cross on the spool and these reels should be put on a horizontal spool pin if possible. Straight wound thread is placed on the spool from top to bottom and these reels are better placed on the vertical spool pin. If you find the thread reel turns too quickly, place a circle of felt underneath it.

For specific advice on machine stitching quilting designs, refer to Finishing: Quilting.

STITCH LENGTH

Getting the stitch length right is important: too small and it can pucker the fabric, slow down the sewing process and be tricky to unpick; too large and it will not hold the seams together securely, the wadding (batting) will be revealed, and the end of the seams could unravel while you are working. Modern machines tend to have a default setting between 2.2mm and 2.4mm (about 10–12 stitches per inch), which is ideal for piecing. If you are sewing fabric together that you are then going to be cutting in to, for improv piecing for example, you may need to adjust the stitch length to a smaller setting so the seams do not unravel when they are cut. When quilting, however, a longer stitch may be required as you are sewing through three layers

If you make a mistake when sewing, use a stitch unpick to cut the thread from the wrong side at regular intervals (every four or five stitches, more often if using a smaller stitch length), then gently pull the fabrics apart and the stitches should break easily.

TROUBLESHOOTING

If your machine is not working properly, read through the manual for advice and try the following:

› Check that it is properly threaded
› Check that the bobbin has been wound correctly
› Change the needle
› Clean the machine, making sure all the lint is removed from the area under the needle plate
› Oil the machine if required

TEMPLATES

Templates are not required every time you sew, for example, square patches can accurately be cut with a rotary cutter and seam lines can be used as a guide for straight line quilting, but there are occasions when they will be needed. These include cutting irregular shapes for piecing, such as quarter circles, preparing patches for English paper piecing, marking designs for appliqué and sometimes for drawing a quilting design if you don't want to sew freehand.

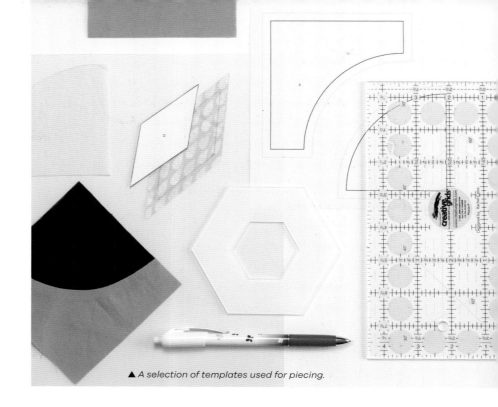

▲ A selection of templates used for piecing.

Ready-Made Templates

Ready-made templates usually come with instructions and are made from sturdy acrylic or plastic so can be used multiple times. Manufacturers often base their templates on traditional designs so these may not suit your project. However, they are ideal for designing work based on standard shapes such as hexagons and circles, and some quilt designers do sell templates made to their own designs. If these are acrylic templates for machine piecing that include seam allowance, they speed up the process as you can simply rotary cut around the acrylic template. For quilting, look out for ready-made stencils that have the design cut out, so you place the whole template on the quilt top and draw along the lines to mark the quilting design.

Making Your Own Templates

If you need a specific design for your project, draft it first either by drawing it onto paper, or designing it using computer software. Alternatively, if you are using one from a pattern make sure you have a copy at the correct size before starting. To be able to draw around the template onto fabric, you will have to make one from template plastic or card. Once made, write the name of the project on the template so it is easy to identify for future use.

Template plastic This transparent material is flexible but strong, so holds its shape well. Simply trace the design, then cut out.

Card This is a cheap, eco-friendly alternative to template plastic. It needs to be thick enough to draw around – if using recycled packaging a cereal packet is ideal. When making a template from shop-bought card, you can photocopy the template straight onto the card. Otherwise, trace it onto layout paper first, using a light box if necessary. Glue the paper copy of the template onto card, then once the glue is dry, carefully cut out along the line. The sides of a card template can wear away if repeatedly drawn around, so it can be a good idea to prepare several.

SEAM ALLOWANCE

Whether to add seam allowance onto a template depends on what you are using it for, so refer to your pattern. With English paper piecing and appliqué, you will not add this as the fabric is cut a distance away from the edge of the template; however, for machine piecing you will need to add ¼in onto each side of your template. For straight lines use the markings on your acrylic ruler, and on curved edges draw dots at small intervals ¼in away from the line, then join together. Alternatively, use a seam wheel. This is a small tool that has a hole in the centre for a pencil, then the wheel spins next to the template to add seam allowance on.

Cutting Fabric Using a Template

Before starting, check your template does not need reversing. Depending on what you are sewing, and if you are marking the right or wrong side of the fabric, it may need to be used upside down. Read the instructions and test beforehand (write a note on top of the template if you will be using it many times).

Place the template on the fabric and draw around it using a pencil designed for use on fabric that will wash out (a sharp point is desirable). If you are drawing on a piece of fabric and experiencing drag, place a piece of fine sandpaper under the fabric to help grip it in place. For piecing and appliqué, cut along the marked lines using scissors or, if you can align your ruler with the marked line, a rotary cutter. For quilting, sew along the marked lines.

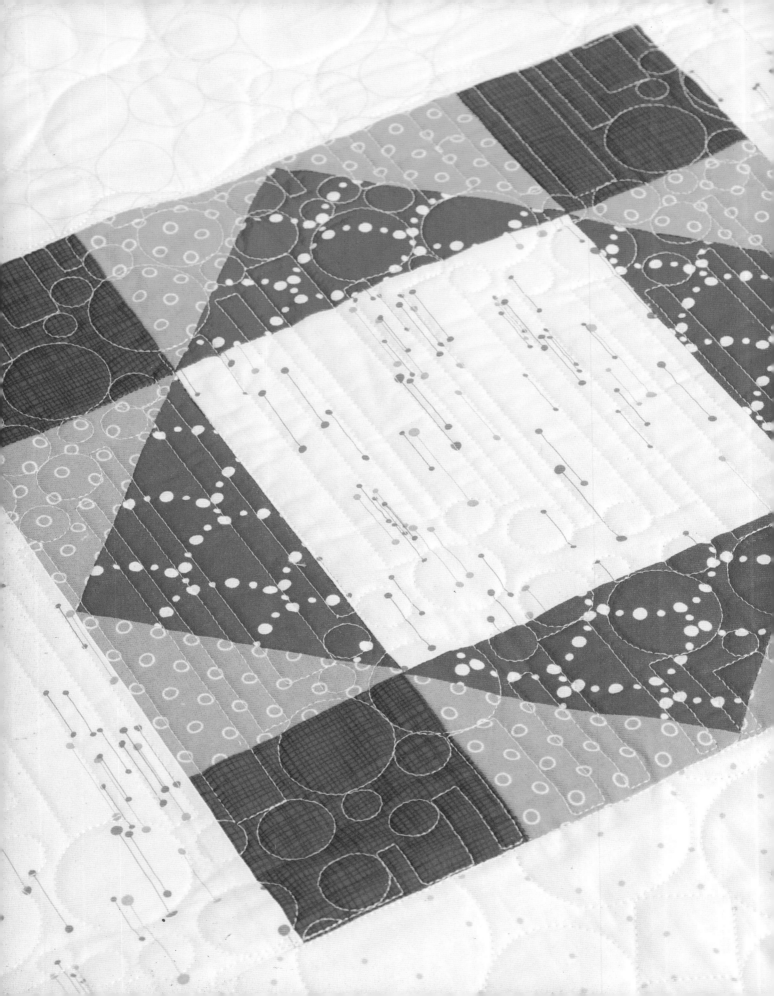

PIECING

Piecing is the term given to the process of joining pieces of fabric together to make a patchwork panel, for a quilt top for example. The section opens with patchwork basics, including essential information on rotary cutting fabric and seam allowance, then the hand-sewn English paper piecing method is described, followed by a wide variety of machine piecing techniques, including basic shapes such as squares as well as improv piecing. There are many different ways to make a piece of patchwork, and the one that you choose will depend on lots of factors including your personal preference and the design of the quilt you are making.

PATCHWORK BASICS

This section covers the basics, so if you are new to patchwork you will find this part particularly useful. Precise cutting, using an accurate seam allowance and good pressing mean that your project should fit together like a jigsaw puzzle. Also included is the speedy machine sewing technique of chain piecing.

Rotary Cutting Patchwork Fabric

When preparing pieces for patchwork piecing, while you can cut fabric by drawing a line and cutting along it with scissors, it is far quicker and more accurate to use a rotary cutter. A set containing a self-healing mat, rotary cutter and ruler is an investment, but if looked after should last a long time, and the only items you will need to buy are replacement blades for your cutter when they start to blunt.

If you are new to using these tools, start off by cutting squares to get used to the technique, such as how hard to push down on the rotary cutter, for example. Remember that the rotary cutter has a circular blade so it is important to take care when using one as accidents can occur. Each time you finish cutting, cover the blade immediately and always store rotary cutters out of the reach of children. Use an acrylic ruler that is thick enough to prevent the blade sliding on top of the ruler and cut away from you in one movement; if you miss a small section, go back and cut with a small pair of scissors. Also, make sure your fingers are not at or over the edge of the ruler when you cut. If you feel the ruler slip when you cut, apply non-slip pads to its underside to help it grip onto the fabric. Remember, you can stop cutting halfway up a piece of fabric, move your hands up, then continue to cut. Don't rush – the more experienced you get in cutting, the more instinctive it will be, and in time this becomes a quick and enjoyable process.

ROTARY CUTTING SQUARES FROM A SINGLE LAYER OF FABRIC

1 Press your fabric and lay it on the cutting mat. Place the ruler on the side of the fabric, with one of the straight lines following the bottom (straight edge) of the fabric. Make sure there is a small amount of material beyond the ruler, then cut. This gives you a straight edge (A).

2 Spin the board (or lift up the fabric) to rotate it 180-degrees. Place the ruler on the fabric. Position the line of the ruler that has the measurement you need along the edge of the fabric. Double check it is straight, then cut. This gives you a strip that is the required width (B).

3 Rotate the strip 90-degrees. Place a straight line of the ruler along one of the cut edges with a small amount of material beyond the ruler, then cut. This gives you perfect right-angled edge (C).

4 Rotate the strip 180-degrees. Position the line of the ruler that has the measurement you need along the edge of the fabric, and a straight line along the bottom of the strip, then cut. This gives you a square. Repeat cutting squares from the strip until you run out of fabric (D).

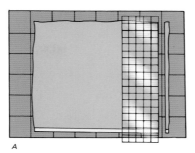

A

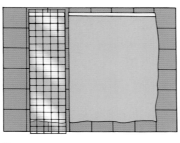

B

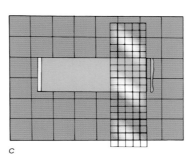

C

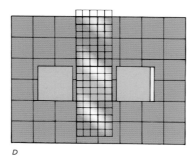

D

ROTARY CUTTING FROM MULTIPLE LAYERS OF FABRIC

You can also cut layers of fabric at a time, either by stacking different fabrics or by folding a large piece of fabric. Be aware that the more layers of fabric you cut, the less likely you are to get a smooth cut and accurate pieces. However, if you have a sharp blade, this method is great for cutting lots of pieces very quickly. It can help to press the fabrics first so they adhere to one another. If using more than four layers of fabric, test first to check cutting accuracy. The method is exactly the same as cutting a single layer of fabric, except crucially the fabric layers remain on the board throughout and only the board is spun around in between the cutting stages. Try to avoid picking up the fabric as the cut edges may not realign.

Tips for Rotary Cutting

› Remember the old saying, 'measure twice, cut once'. Always take the time to double check your measurements.

› If cutting long strips using a long rectangular ruler, use the length rather than the width. If cutting strips longer than your mat you can fold the fabric first.

› Replace the blade as soon as it starts to blunt. Keep a set of spare blades in your kit so you always have one to hand.

› The first time you change the blade, take photos or a video of the disassembly stages to make reassembly easier. The blades are sharp, so be careful when handling them, and discard used blades safely.

› Always use your rotary cutter with a self-healing mat. In between use, store your mat flat and away from heat: if stored on its side, a mat can warp, making it impossible to cut a straight line.

› Keep one side of your mat for cutting wadding (batting), saving the other side for cutting fabric, as the wadding can get in the cutting grooves. Clean your mat by running a magic sponge, dampening it a little if necessary, along any lint stuck to the board.

Machine Piecing

Sewing with an accurate seam allowance and pressing fabric well are essential elements for putting together a well-made quilt.

CHECKING SEAM ALLOWANCE

Before starting a project, you will need to check the seam allowance to be used. The majority of patchwork is sewn with a ¼in seam. A special foot is available for most machines that makes it easy to achieve the correct width (see Sewing Basics: Machine Sewing Basics – The Quarter-Inch Foot).

TESTING THE SEAM ALLOWANCE

When machine piecing for patchwork, it is essential to use an accurate ¼in seam allowance, otherwise your patches will not fit together. When working with a new sewing machine, or if you have started your project and your seams are not meeting as they should, it is a good idea to check your seam allowance. Cut four 2 x 4in strips and sew their long sides together. Press, then measure. The piece should be 6½ x 4in. If it is larger than this, your seam allowance needs to be increased; if smaller, then it is too generous.

MAKING YOUR OWN SEAM GUIDE

If you haven't got a ¼in-foot there are a couple of ways of achieving an accurate seam allowance. One way is to line a piece of scrap fabric up with the edge of a standard presser foot, sew about 4in then take the fabric out and measure the distance between the edge of the fabric and the sewn line. If it is not ¼in, move the position of your needle by changing the width on your sewing machine. Test again, and then keep doing this till you have it right. Make a note of what position it should be in with a sticky memo note. If you cannot move the needle width on your machine, use the same method but stick a strip of low-tack masking tape on the sewing machine ¼in away from your needle, align the fabric next to this and test the position, moving it slightly until it is right. You can also buy seam guides that fix onto your machine that work in the same way.

SCANT QUARTER-INCH SEAM ALLOWANCE

Patterns sometimes refer to using a scant ¼in seam allowance. This means taking a tiny fraction less than a ¼in and is used when accuracy is important where even the tiny amount of fabric lost in the bulk of the thread and pressing of the seam allowance can affect the pattern. If you are using a ¼in seam allowance but your piecing is still not coming up quite right, then try taking a scant ¼in seam allowance and see if this makes a difference.

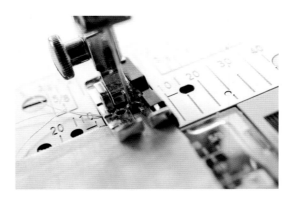

▲ A ¼-inch foot.

CHAIN PIECING

Chain piecing is a technique where you keep sewing pieces of fabric together on an assembly line, without cutting the thread in between pieces. It is quick and can save on thread.

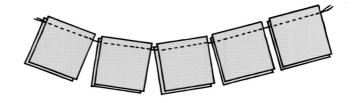

1 Line up two pieces of fabric, right sides together. Place them under the presser foot, just before the needle.

2 Hold the threads to the back, and sew along the seam, making sure to guide (not pull) the fabric through the machine.

3 When you get to the end of the fabric, stop sewing with the needle down. Lift the presser foot and lay the next piece of fabric to be sewn about ⅛in away.

4 Lower the presser foot and carefully start sewing again. There should be a couple of stitches sewn between the fabric pieces.

5 Continue sewing, feeding pieces through in the same way. When you have finished sewing, take the line of fabric pieces from the machine and cut the threads in between them.

Pressing

Sometimes overlooked, good pressing is vital to making a well-made quilt. Before starting, if fabric has been pressed it is much easier to cut accurately; and while piecing, pressing each seam means that you should end up with a piece of patchwork that does not distort. Make sure you store your iron somewhere clean. If using products such as fusible web, which can stick to the iron and cause grubby marks, place a piece of baking paper or calico between the fabric and the iron to act as a pressing mat. Remember to clean your iron regularly.

HOW TO PRESS SEAMS

For best results when working on piecing make sure you press using a dry iron (no steam) in an up and down motion, rather than side to side, as heat relaxes the fibres in the fabric so moving the iron can cause them to move and distort.

After sewing the seam, press the fabric with wrong sides still together (this helps the fabric threads settle in place), then open the fabric and press using your preferred method (refer to To Press Seams Open or Together). Whichever way you choose, make sure your seams are flat: if you leave a small piece of fabric in the fold, then the measurements won't work. If you have a long seam, lift the iron up and down as you work your way along it.

An iron is not always necessary for pressing. If you are working on a project with fabric that is easy to press, for example, foundation piecing with cotton, then you can finger press or use a seam roller if you prefer.

TO PRESS SEAMS OPEN OR TOGETHER

Quilters tend to have a preference for pressing, however this can change depending on what type of piecing they are working on.

PRESSING SEAMS OPEN

Place the fabric on an ironing board or pressing mat wrong side up. Carefully open the seam with your fingers (or use a stiletto tool to protect your fingers), then press. Allow to cool, then press from the front, checking the seam is neat and flat.

The advantages of pressing this way are:

› The fabric lies flatter, so is good for lighter fabrics such as cotton lawn where the ridge of the seam allowance could show from the front.
› Where lots of seams meet in the same place, the bulk can be evenly distributed.
› If working with two light fabrics, then any seam allowance that can be seen through the front of the fabric will look even throughout the quilt.

› A flatter quilt top can also be easier to quilt: for example, if a fabric such as denim was pressed with seams facing the same way, it would create a ridge for the sewing machine foot to go over when machine quilting.

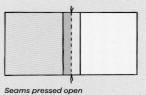

Seams pressed open

PRESSING SEAMS FACING THE SAME WAY

Place the fabric on an ironing board or pressing mat right side up. Place the dark fabric (or the one you want the seam to sit behind) to the back. Hold this up with one hand, while pressing along the seam with the other. This will push the seams together and ensure the seam is neat and flat.

The advantages of pressing this way are:

› It is a much quicker way of pressing compared to pressing seams open.
› As the seam is not being pulled in opposite directions there is less strain on the seam. This means that the wadding (batting) is less likely to work its way through the seams (known as 'bearding') as there are no gaps between stitches.
› Certain piecing techniques, such as squares, use the bulk created from pressing to one side to an advantage

› If a light fabric is pressed towards a darker fabric this disguises the seam allowance.
› A ridge is created that can be helpful if you are quilting in the ditch.

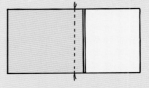

Seams pressed facing the same way

ENGLISH PAPER PIECING

English paper piecing, also known as mosaic patchwork, is a technique where the fabric is wrapped around a paper template to make individual patches. These are then hand sewn together before removing the tacking (basting) stitches and papers to leave a patchwork panel or quilt top. It is ideal for sewing complex shapes, such as hexagons (these have Y-seams, so need careful thought before machine sewing), although many people just enjoy the repetitive action that hand sewing brings.

Preparing Paper Templates

To start, you will need a template that is the finished size (does not include seam allowance). This can either be a ready-made or make-it-yourself template (see Sewing Basics: Templates). Using a fine pencil, draw around the template onto lightweight paper (photocopy weight is ideal) as many times as the fabric patches you require for your design. Cut out carefully just inside the line – it is important to be fairly accurate as the paper patches need to be the same size so they fit together. If working with a regular shape, you can often buy pre-cut papers, which means you can skip this stage and move straight on to tacking (basting).

TACKING (BASTING) FABRIC AROUND A PAPER TEMPLATE

1 Pin a paper template to the wrong side of a piece of fabric. Cut out the fabric around the template leaving a generous ¼in seam allowance (A).

2 Starting along one side, fold the excess fabric over the paper, then sew tacking (basting) stitches through the paper and fabric, working your way around the shape, folding the corners as you go (B). Note, when you tack (baste) around shapes with sharp points, such as triangles, you will create 'ears' from the excess fabric at the points (C) – do not trim them.

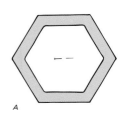

A

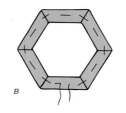

B

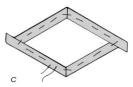

C

As an alternative to tacking (basting) use a fabric glue stick (sparingly) to adhere the fabric over the patches.

Joining Fabric Patches

Once all your fabric patches are tacked (basted), lay them out in your design, ready to join them together. The process of joining can depend on your design, but usually the patches are joined in smaller sections then sewn together at the end. This means the project is portable, and there is less strain on the outer edges of the patchwork as you work.

1 Thread a needle with a toning thread, but don't put a knot in the end. Pick up two patches that are next to each other and place them right sides together. Push the needle through the folded edge about ¼in from the corner on the side you will start stitching (this can be to the left or the right depending on your preference). Pull the thread through, leaving a tail approximately ½in long (A).

2 Put a finger on the thread tail to hold it in place, then take small whip stitches back to the corner, keeping a hold on the thread tail. Try not to stitch through the papers, just through the fabric at the folded edges (B).

3 When you get to the corner, stitch back along the seam, catching the thread tail in the stitching. When you get to the other corner, take several stitches back along the seam, in the same way as when you started (C). Two fabric patches have now been joined (D).

4 Continue to join the patches into sections, and the sections into the complete panel/quilt top. If you are sewing a long seam and run out of thread, stop and finish thread in the same way as when you start and finish a patch. When you have finished, press the patchwork with a medium iron, then carefully unpick the tacking (basting) stitches and remove the paper templates out the back.

If you prefer, you can secure the start of the stitching with a knot hidden in the fold of the fabric, then finish off with a small knot.

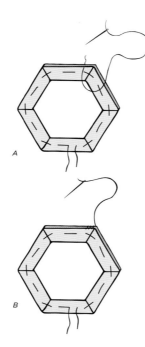

A

B

C

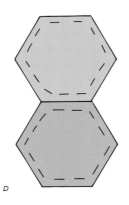

D

Tips for English Paper Piecing

› Some quilters prefer to use ladder stitch to whip stitch when joining patches or sections as it gives a less visible finish.

› You may find you have to fold the patchwork to get it in the right position to sew additional patches. This is fine – don't be afraid to fold and manipulate the paper.

› Sometimes, even if you have cut and stitched accurately, the fabric may distort slightly and you may find that a patch is slightly bigger than the space it is to be sewn to; if so, you can ease the fabric a little to make it fit.

› When sewing a triangle into a V-shaped space, start at an outer edge and work towards the point. Curves can be English paper pieced, too. Take your time, and clip into the seam allowance if needed; you may also want to make a mark on the paper to denote the halfway point of each patch to ensure they fit as they should.

› A faster way of making a quilt top using English paper piecing is to work with larger shapes.

› For a less formal geometric layout you can easily make your own design by dividing up a piece of paper with straight lines. Then number the patches and photocopy it to refer to when piecing, then cut up the original and use the papers as templates.

Finishing the Quilt Top

The irregular edges can cause issues when it comes to finishing off English paper piecing. Here are some options for you to explore.

APPLIQUÉ TO BACKGROUND FABRIC

Whether it is a 10in piece or a whole quilt top, a panel of English paper piecing can be sewn onto a background fabric.

1 If the fabric patches have 'ears', these need to be tucked behind the patchwork when sewing it to the background. Alternatively, you can tuck the ears in when you tack (baste) the fabric around the paper templates before joining, so the edges are already neat (A).

2 Lay out the backing fabric, then pin the paper pieced panel to it (small appliqué pins are handy for this) and slip stitch around the edge (B).

3 It is often easier to remove the papers *after* the panel has been applied to the background, by cutting a slit in the backing fabric through which to extract them. But if you do not want two layers of fabric – for example, if the backing shadows through the patchwork fabrics, or if you only want one layer so it is easier to hand quilt – then you can cut away the backing fabric a generous ¼in inside the hand-sewn line (C).

If you prefer, you can remove the papers before sewing in place – just give the patchwork a good press with some starch so the edges hold their shape, then hand or machine sew in place.

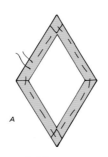

A

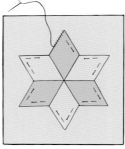

B

C

▲ *An English paper pieced star appliquéd to a background fabric.*

PIECED TO STRAIGHTEN

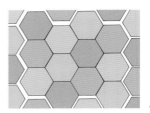

A

An easy way to finish with a straight edge is to use patches that are cropped from your main shape. To do this, look at how the pattern would need straightening around the edge, then copy your template and trim it down to make the shape required. Tack (baste) and sew as before to end up with a straight edge. You may need to make several different new templates to fill in the gaps at the edge (A).

TRIMMING THE SIDES

A

If the side of the panel is being bound, then you can just trim the piece – you do not need to worry about the edges as they will be neatened. However, if you wish to add a machine-sewn border, then you need to flip out the seam allowance around the edge of the pieced panel, then trim the sides. After taking out the template papers from the edging shapes, lay the folded edge flat, then cut ¼in away from the fold to make a straight line (A). Machine sew the border using a ⅜in seam allowance; this means you lose a tiny part of the points at the edge of your design, but ensures that no holes appear in the seam where the hand sewing seam was finished.

SQUARES AND STRIPS

Patchwork made from squares, rectangles and strips is usually straightforward to sew and therefore a quick and satisfying way to make a quilt. Used simply, they can showcase a bold print or colour layout and a quick graphic-looking quilt can be made – take a favourite fabric, mix it with a couple of other prints or plains, then cut long strips at different widths and sew them together. Alternatively, they can be made into a much more visually and technically complex design, such as a pixellated image.

Joining Squares

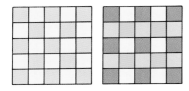

The technique below describes pressing the rows with the seams facing the same way to create a ridge that is used to help align the seams, but if you prefer you can press the seams open.

Sizing notes Cut your squares ½in larger than the finished size to allow for seam allowance.

This method is the same for sewing together squares that have been pieced, for example half-square triangles.

1 Cut as many squares as required and lay them out on a surface or place them on a design wall (A).

2 Using ¼in seam allowance sew the squares together into rows, then press seams facing the same way in alternate directions, so rows 1, 3 and 5 face to the right, and rows 2, 4 to the left (B) (or press open if you prefer).

3 Take the top two rows and place them right sides together. Line up the squares ready to pin at each seam intersection. Place two seams opposite each other and gently move until you can feel where the ridge created by pressing the seams in alternate directions makes the fabric 'lock' together. When happy the seams are adjacent, pin to hold (C). (If you have pressed the seams open the pin will be level with the seam.) Sew the rows together, removing the pins just before they go under the sewing machine needle. Continue to join each row in turn until all the rows have been joined.

A

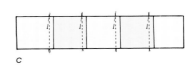

B

C

Quick Square Method

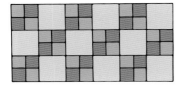 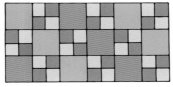 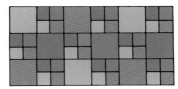

This is an ideal method if you need lots of squares. In this example, it has been used to make four-patch units that are combined with larger squares. The technique is easy to adjust, for example, you could join three, four or more strips together before cutting units.

MAKING THE FOUR-PATCH UNITS

Sizing notes Cut your strips ½in wider than the finished square size required, and when cutting them down cut the units to the same size as the width. For example, for each square to be 3in when finished, cut 3½in wide strips. Once sewn together, cut 3½in wide sets of squares from the sewn strip.

1 Cut a strip from each of the fabrics for the small squares (A).

2 Sew the strips together using a ¼in seam allowance (B). Press the seam open or towards the darker fabric depending on your preference.

3 Place the strip on your cutting mat. If needed, trim one end so it is square, then cut sets of squares from the strip (C).

4 Take two sets of squares and rotate one of them. Place them right sides together, pin the central seam so it is aligned, then sew (D). Open the unit and press (E). Repeat this process to make as many units as you require.

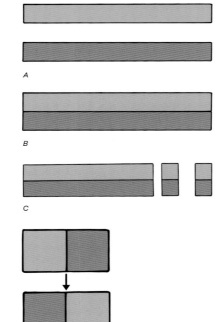

CUTTING THE LARGE SQUARES AND JOINING FOUR-PATCH UNITS

Sizing notes The large squares need to be the finished size of two small squares plus ½in. For example, for 3in small squares finished, cut 6½in large squares.

1 Cut your large squares and lay them out, alternating them with the pieced units (A).

2 Sew the units together into rows, press, then sew the rows together (B). Repeat to join all the rows.

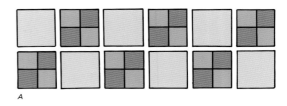

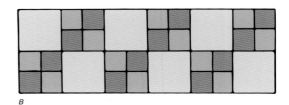

Triangular Corners for Squares and Strips

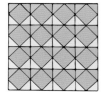 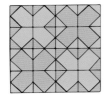 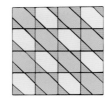

Designs can be created by adding a triangle on each corner (see method below), or on two or three corners only. If your fabric is distorting, give the foundation piecing method a try.

A SQUARE IN A SQUARE

Sizing notes The large square is the finished size plus ½in. Corner squares are half the finished size of the centre square plus ½in for seam allowance. For example, for 5in square finished, cut one 5½in large square and four 3in small squares.

1 Cut one large square and four small squares. On the wrong side of the four small squares draw a diagonal line from corner to corner (A).

2 Place one small square on a corner of the large square, wrong sides together and outer edges aligned (B).

3 Sew along the marked line. Trim the fabric ¼in away from the sewn line (C), then flip open the corner and press.

4 Place another small square on an adjacent corner, wrong sides together and outer edges aligned (D) and repeat step 3.

5 Repeat step 4 to sew the last two small squares to the remaining corners (E).

If you flip open a corner and find it is not lining up, try sewing just next to the drawn line.

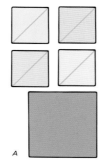

A

B

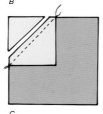

C

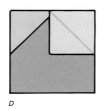

D

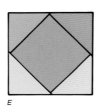

E

VARIATIONS ON A SQUARE WITH TRIANGULAR CORNERS

By changing the size of the small corner squares being sewn to the large central one, this method can also be used to create units that look very different (F–H).

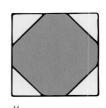 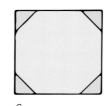 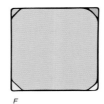

F   G   H

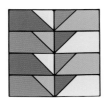 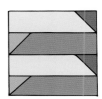

TRIANGLE ON THE END OF A STRIP

This nifty technique can create really interesting irregular units. The length of the strip will depend on your design.

Sizing notes The corner square needs to be the width of the strip. For example, for a 3in wide strip finished, cut a 3½in wide strip and a 3½in square.

1 Cut a strip and a square. On the wrong side of the square draw a diagonal line from corner to corner. Place the square on the end of the strip, right sides together (A), and sew along the marked line.

2 Trim the fabric ¼in away from the drawn line (B).

3 Flip open the corner and press the seam open or towards the darker fabric depending on your preference (C).

A

B

C

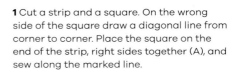

Bricks

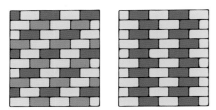

Off-set rectangles with a square at the end makes an easy quilt as, unlike squares, there are no seam intersections to match.

STAGGERED BLOCKS

Sizing notes Cut bricks and half-bricks ½in larger than the finished size. For example, for 3 x 6in bricks finished, cut 3½ x 6½in strips and 3½in squares.

1 Cut as many strips and squares as required and lay them out on a surface or design wall, alternating between a row starting with a square and ending with a square (A).

2 Using a ¼in seam allowance, sew the pieces together to make rows (B). Press the seams open or towards the darker fabric depending on your preference.

3 Take the top two rows. With right sides together line them up and pin at each end. If necessary, add more pins along the row. Sew rows together with a ¼in seam allowance and press seams as preferred (C). Repeat to join all the rows.

A

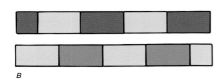

B

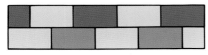

C

Strip Blocks

These are versatile and can create really interesting effects if colour principles such as grading from light to dark are applied to the fabric selection. Alternatively, this would work well with ombre fabric. The method described here sub-cuts into squares, but it can easily be adapted to make rectangular-shaped units.

CHECKERBOARD EFFECT

Sizing notes If sewing strips to sub-cut into blocks, then divide the size of the block by how many strips and add on seam allowance. For example, for a 12in finished block made of six strips each strip will be 2in wide finished, so cut strips 2½in wide. The width of the block will be 12½in, so the strips needs to be multiples of this. So, for three of these blocks you will need strips at least 37½in long.

1 Cut strips and lay them out in a pleasing order. Sew the strips together one at a time with right sides together, pressing seams open or towards the darker fabric depending on your preference (A).

2 If needed, trim the end so it is straight, then cut squares from the strips to create blocks (B).

3 Lay out the squares in a checkerboard design, sew them together into rows, then sew the rows together (C).

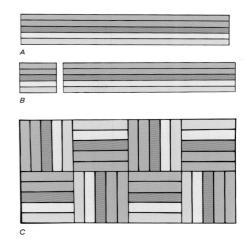

A

B

C

Tips for Working with Strips

Long wide strips make a simple, easy-to-piece quilt top – a good way to show off a special fabric or experiment with quilting, but there are some technical issues:

› Be aware of whether the strip has been cut on the width or the length of the fabric. If cut on the width it is more likely to stretch or bow.

› If you are sewing lots of long strips together, start sewing at one end for seam 1 and the opposite end for seam 2, and alternate each time to even out the tension.

› One way to prevent the fabric from stretching is to cut it to the exact size required and pin before sewing to make sure it fits.

› Fold long strips of fabric to mark the half and/or quarter sections, and start by pinning them together at these points to make sure the fabrics are evenly distributed.

TRIANGLES

These three-sided shapes can be used in a simple arrangement on their own, or mixed and matched with other shapes such as squares or rectangles, leading to a huge number of options when designing and making quilts. The methods given in this section are for quick techniques but do remember that units such as half-square triangles and quarter-square triangles can be cut one patch at a time using a template – good for complex designs that use lots of fabrics.

Tips for Working with Triangles

› Triangle units are easy to sew but can result in technical issues due to at least one side of the shape being cut on the bias. To prevent the fabric stretching or distorting, be aware of the grain; sew and press units gently (refer to Patchwork Basics: Machine Piecing), and if necessary use starch.

› When making half-square triangles, some quilters like to use a printed template sheet. This has the sewing and cutting lines marked on and is placed on the back of the fabric to use as a guide. It is sewn through, then torn away at the end.

› If sewing fabric ¼in away from a drawn line, you can either use a ¼in foot, or mark the line then use a standard presser foot to follow it.

› When working with triangles you will often have seam allowance peeking out at the end of the line of sewing. These little points, widely known as 'ears', are usually trimmed, although for some techniques, such as equilateral triangles, they can be used to align patches when sewing.

› Some methods for sewing triangles cut away fabric that is not required, so you are left with off-cuts. You could sew these together to make a batch of small units suitable for a small project.

› Triangles can look eye-catching when made with a directional fabric and you can create easy optical effects, but before cutting consider the direction of the print and the angle of the triangle to make sure the fabric pattern is facing the way you wish.

Half-Square Triangles (HST)

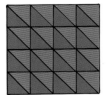 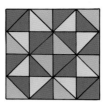

Sizing notes Cut your squares ⅞in larger than your finished size. Alternatively, if you would rather trim them to size at the end cut them 1¼in larger. So, for a 3in finished square, you will cut either 3⅞in or 4¼in squares.

CUTTING SQUARES TO MAKE HST UNITS

1 Cut squares from at least two different fabrics and on each one cut across the diagonal from corner to corner (A).

2 Take two different fabric triangles, place them right sides together and sew using a ¼in seam allowance (B).

3 Open the unit, pressing the seam open or towards the darker fabric depending on your preference (C).

A

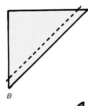

B

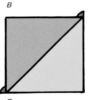

C

MAKING TWO HST UNITS AT A TIME

1 Cut one square each from two different fabrics. On the wrong side of the lighter square draw a diagonal line from corner to corner. Place the two squares right sides together with the lighter square on top and align their edges.

2 Sew ¼in away from the drawn line on each side (A).

3 Cut along the central line to make two units (B). Open the units, pressing the seam open or towards the darker fabric depending on your preference (C).

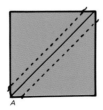

A

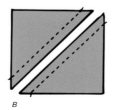

B

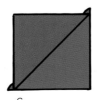

C

MAKING EIGHT HST UNITS AT A TIME

Sizing notes To work out the size of your squares take the finished size of one HST and add ⅞in, then multiply by two. So, for 3in HST finished add ⅞in to 3in = 3⅞in. Then multiply by two to get a total of 7¾in, so cut your squares to this size. If you wish to make them larger so they can be trimmed to size, add on another ½in to the total.

1 On the wrong side of your palest fabric draw two diagonal lines from corner to corner. Then draw a vertical and horizontal line across the centre (A).

2 Sew ¼in away from each side of the drawn diagonal lines (B).

3 Press the fabric then cut along the diagonal, vertical and horizontal lines (C).

4 Open the units, pressing the seam open or toward the darker fabric depending on your preference (D).

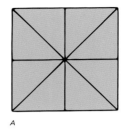

A

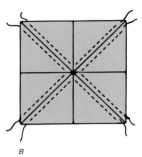

B

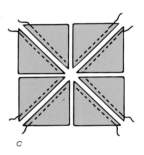

C

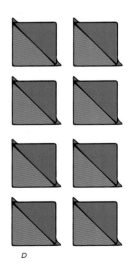

D

TRIMMING DOWN HST UNITS

Due to the issues created when sewing on the bias, HST units can sometimes finish slightly different to the measurement you require. If you make them larger, they can then be trimmed down to the exact size, particularly important if you are mixing the units with other shapes such as squares. Remember to include your seam allowance in the measurements, so if your project needs a 6in finished unit you need to trim it to 6½in square.

TRIMMING HST UNIT WITH A STANDARD RULER

You will need a ruler with a 45-degree line that finishes in a corner, or you can draw the line, or mark it with a piece of tape. The ruler needs to be the same size as, or larger than, the size of the required square.

1 Press the unit and place it right-side up on your cutting mat. Align the 45-degree line of the ruler with the seam line across the middle of the HST. Position the top of the ruler so there is a small amount of excess fabric at the top and side (A).

2 Cut up the side and along the top and remove the ruler. You should now have a neat right angle at one corner with the seam going right to the very corner (B).

3 Turn the unit 180-degrees and repeat step 2, however, this time line up the desired measurement of your ruler on the side and bottom of the unit (C).

4 When you are happy the measurement is correct, and the seam line is correctly positioned through the centre, cut the top and side then remove the ruler (D).

5 You should now have a neat square with the diagonal seam running from corner to corner (E).

You can use a specialist ruler to trim a HST unit before it is pressed open. These have a line that is placed on the stitch line, then the excess cut away. Follow the manufacturer's instructions.

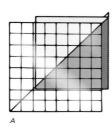

A

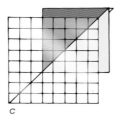

B

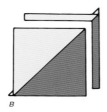

C

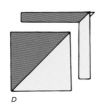

D

E

Quarter-Square Triangles (QST)

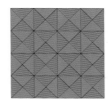
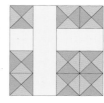
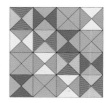

Sizing notes Cut your squares 1¼in larger than the finished size. For example, for a 6in square finished, cut 7¼in squares.

CUTTING SQUARES TO MAKE QST UNITS

1 Make two HST units (see Making Two HST Units at a Time, steps 1 and 2). Open up the units and press. If the seams are pressed together, towards the darker fabric, then they will 'nest' in step 3. Cut across each HST unit on the diagonal from corner to corner in the opposite direction to the seam (A). Repeat with another set of HST units.

2 Swap one piece from each side (B).

3 Place the units right sides together. Pin at the centre, so the seams meet, and at each end, then sew using ¼in seam allowance. Open and press (C).

A

B

C

◀ *This design combines half-square triangles and squares.*

Flying Geese

 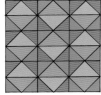 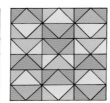

MAKING ONE FLYING GEESE UNIT AT A TIME

Sizing notes Cut your rectangle ½in larger than the finished size and the squares ½in larger than the finished width. For example, for a 6 x 3in rectangle unit finished, cut a 6½ x 3½in rectangle and two 3½in squares.

1 Cut a rectangle and two squares. On the wrong side of the two squares, draw a diagonal line from corner to corner (A).

2 Place one square on the side of the rectangle, right sides together and aligning edges as shown. The diagonal line should run from an outer corner towards the centre of the rectangle (B). Pin and flip to check it is how you want it to be (especially important if using a directional fabric). Carefully sew along the marked line.

3 Cut the fabric ¼in from the sewn line (C).

4 Open the corner and press (D).

5 Follow steps 2 and 3 to sew the remaining square on the opposite corner (E).

6 Flip open the corner and press. Your flying geese unit is complete (F).

A

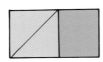

B

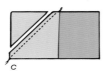

C

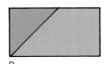

D

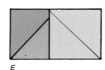

E

F

These flying geese methods work with units that are of the ratio 1:2, so finished size 4 x 8in or 5½ x 11in. For elongated flying geese, use the foundation piecing method (see Foundation Piecing).

MAKING FOUR FLYING GEESE UNITS AT A TIME

Sizing notes The large squares which make up the large triangles are cut the width of the finished flying geese unit plus 1¼in, and the small squares which are the background are the finished width of the flying geese units plus ⅞in. For example, for a 6 x 3in rectangle unit finished, cut one 7¼in large square and four 3⅞in small squares.

1 Cut one large square and four small squares. Draw a diagonal line on the wrong side of each of the small squares, from corner to corner (A).

2 Take two of the squares and place them at opposite corners of the large square, right sides together (B).

3 Sew ¼in from the drawn lines on each side (C).

4 Cut along the centre line to make two units (D).

5 Taking one unit, flip open the small triangles and press (E).

6 Place a small square on top of the pressed unit, right sides together and aligning two sides as shown. Sew ¼in either side of the drawn line (F).

7 Cut along the line to make two units (G).

8 Press the corners open to make two flying geese units (H).

9 Repeat steps 5–8 with the remaining unit and square to make another two flying geese.

A

B

C

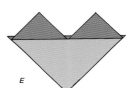

D

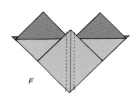

E

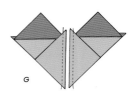

F

G

H

Equilateral Triangles

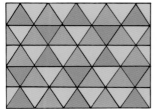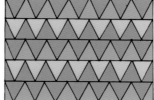

Sizing notes Cut your strip ¾in wider than the height of your finished triangle. For example, for 3in tall finished triangles, cut a 3¾in wide strip. With this method, the panel is trimmed to size at the end.

1 This method uses a standard rectangular ruler with a 60-degree line marked on each end. Cut a strip to the desired size, then place the 60-degree marking on your ruler along the top straight right-hand edge, with the end of the line level with the top corner of the fabric strip cut (A).

2 Rotate the ruler and slide it to the bottom of the strip to line up the 60-degree line as before, then cut (B).

3 Continue in this way, alternating the triangles to cut the strip (C).

4 Place two triangles right sides together. Sew down one side using ¼in seam allowance (D). Flip open; press the seam open (E).

5 Place the next triangle right sides facing on the end of the row. Align the edge so it is level with the previous piece: you will find the fabric of the new piece is longer on one edge, so make sure this aligns with the ear at one end of the previous seam. Repeat, sewing and pressing each piece to form the rows (F).

6 To sew rows together, place a pin at each intersection, going through both points to help them meet. After sewing, trim the edges square.

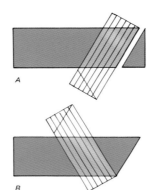

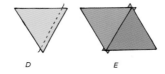

If sewing lots of these, look out for specialist equilateral triangle rulers – these make it easy to cut and sew and have instructions to help with accurate sizing.

Half-Rectangle Triangles

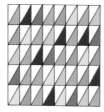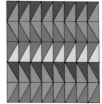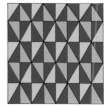

Sizing notes Templates are used to ensure the rectangle is the desired size.

1 Draw a rectangle at the finished size and divide in half diagonally. Trace one half onto template plastic and draw a line ¼in away from the diagonal edge, and ½in away from the two straight edges. At the two ends of the diagonal edge, line the ruler up with the line and draw ½in beyond the point. Cut, following the outer line (A). Repeat with the second half of the rectangle.

2 Use the templates to cut your fabric and sew using ¼in seam allowance (B). Once sewn, open the unit and press.

3 Take a piece of clear template plastic (or tracing paper) and draw the finished size rectangle. Then draw a diagonal line across the middle to mark the seam. Next, draw another line ¼in away from the outer line for your seam allowance and cut (C).

4 Place the template on top (right side) of the unit, lining up the diagonal line with the seam, and cut (D).

5 The seams at the corner look slightly off; this allows for the seam allowance when joining units together (E).

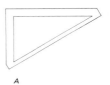

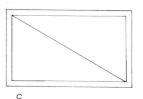

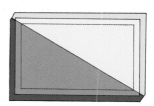

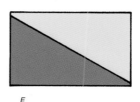

The diagonal seam line can face left or right so check you have drawn your line as required before cutting.

CURVED PIECING

The use of curves in quilt design can result in intriguing designs that have a playful sense of pattern and movement. They look trickier to sew than they actually are, and it is fairly easy to make your own templates by using a compass or household item, such as a plate, then add a ¼in seam allowance onto each piece, including the curved edges. If you buy an acrylic template, then the patches can be cut using a small rotary cutter. The machine-sewn techniques described in this section are based on fabric cut using a template that includes seam allowance, but they can also be sewn using hand techniques.

Orange Peel

The orange peel shape has a lovely retro feel to it, and when multiple blocks are joined together it results in a graphic-looking design. The block can create an interesting effect if the peel shape is used as the background rather than the frame.

If you are new to these techniques, start with a larger (over 6in square) design as it can get trickier when working with smaller shapes.

1 Using a template cut out one convex unit and two concave units (A).

2 Referring to Quarter Circles, steps 2–5, sew one concave side unit to the convex centre and press open (B).

3 Repeat to add the remaining side unit onto the opposite side of the centre to complete one orange peel unit (C). Note, this diagram shows the ¼in seam allowance around the outside, and when the units are joined together the corner of the peel will finish at the seam.

A

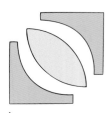

B

C

Quarter Circles

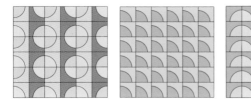

These classic shapes are used in traditional Drunkard's Path blocks but they are incredibly versatile. They can be joined to the end of a long rectangular piece of fabric to create the effect of a frame, and it can be fun to try playing with negative space to create an abstract foreground and background to a design. The outer piece is the concave curve and the inner piece is the convex curve.

▲ *Quarter circles can look interesting when used at corners, as shown in this simple nine-patch block.*

1 Using a template cut out a concave and a convex unit (A).

2 Fold both units in half and finger press or iron the fold (B). Open them up, then place them next to one another, aligning the folds (C).

3 Place the concave unit on top of the convex one, right sides together and lining up the centre creases. Pin at this point (D).

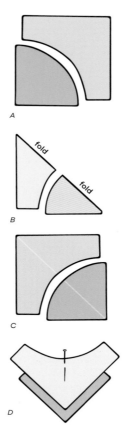

4 Working on one side at a time, align the ends and pin at each end and at the centre point (E). Then place more pins along the edge of the fabric (F).

5 Carefully stitch the two pieces together, removing the pins as you go (G). If you need to adjust the fabric as you stitch, remember to stop stitching with the needle down through the fabric before raising the presser foot. Open the fabric and press the seam open or towards the concave shape depending on your preference (H).

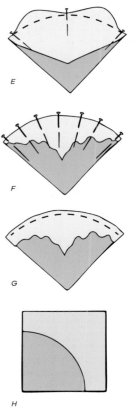

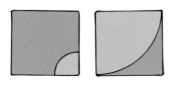

VARIATIONS ON QUARTER CIRCLES

Altering the scale of the quarter circle creates different effects. An interesting quilt can be made using a variety of quarter circle sizes to create a regular, but random look.

PARTIAL AND INSET SEAMS

These are used where it is not possible to join fabric using a continuous seam, such as where three pieces of fabric meet. Instead, the seam is only sewn along the places where the fabric is joined and not into the seam allowance. When machine piecing, it requires a little preparation and interrupts the flow of stitching but is fairly quick to sew. It is easy when hand sewing and the template method described in this section is an alternative to the English paper piecing technique.

Partial Seams

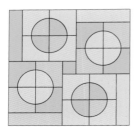

This method is needed when sewing irregular squares, strips or rectangles that cannot be put together with a straight line of stitching. It is a similar method to Inset Seams, but rather than fitting in a shape to two others, you are working on the seams in a methodical way to ensure the piece lays flat. Make sure the fabric is cut to size first, so you are not trying to ease in a larger piece than fits.

1 Take two pieces to be joined and place them right sides together. Sew along the seam, starting about 2in from the end (A). By leaving this unsewn you will be able to join the last piece. If you are working on a large piece (for example, making a quilt made of different sized squares) this seam may be under strain from moving the fabric around so reverse the stitching to secure.

2 Open the bottom half of the strip and press. Then continue sewing the rest of the strips (B).

3 After sewing the last strip return to the first seam and sew from the end (C), overlapping the stitching at the place where you started by about ½in to secure.

A

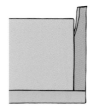

B

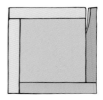

C

Inset Seams

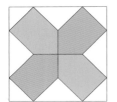
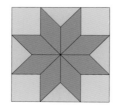

This technique, also referred to as a sewing a Y-seam, is used when piecing a design where three shapes need joining together, such as with hexagons or diamonds.

MARKING METHOD FOR MACHINE PIECING

In this technique, the end of each seam is marked onto the fabric so the stitching does not go into the seam allowance. Use a fabric marker that washes out easily, such as a chalk pencil.

1 On the wrong side of your fabric place a dot or a small line at the beginning and end of where each seam will be sewn (A). If using a plastic or paper template that includes seam allowance, you could use a compass to make a small hole where this dot should go to make marking it easier.

A

2 Place two pieces of fabric right sides together and align their edges. Sew the seams between the marked dots, reverse stitching at the start and finish to secure (B). Do not sew beyond the marked points, otherwise the next shape will not lay flat once it is sewn next to them. Open out and press.

B

3 Take the next fabric piece, place it right sides together with one of the shapes and align the edges. Sew the seam between the dots. Take it from the machine then rearrange so the next part of the seam is aligned, pin, then sew (C). Open out and press, fanning the seams in the middle (D).

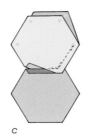

C

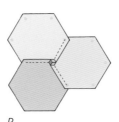

D

TEMPLATE METHOD FOR HAND PIECING

This method of piecing is popular with those who make quilts within the slow stitching ethos. It can be used for any piecing that uses templates, such as triangles or quarter circles, but is really useful as an alternative when sewing inset seams as you are only stitching around the size of the finished shape and not into the seam allowance.

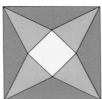
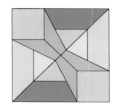

1 Prepare your templates. These will be the finished size and can be cut from card, or from template plastic for more durability. Draw around your template onto the wrong side of your fabric. Cut the fabric ¼in away from the drawn line. Repeat to cut more shapes.

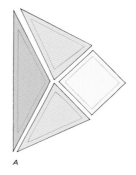

A

2 Take two adjacent shapes and place them right sides together. Place pins through the fabric at the start and finish of the drawn line and at intervals of about 2in (A). Make sure the pin goes through the line on both pieces – you want to make sure they are aligned.

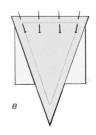

B

3 Thread up a needle and put a knot in the end. Place the needle through the start of the line and take a backstitch (B). Sew a running stitch along the line, taking a backstitch every couple of inches to secure the seam (C). When you reach the end of the line, take two backstitches to secure.

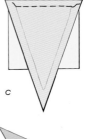

C

4 Open the fabric and continue piecing further patches in the same way (D). When joining one piece to another that has a previously sewn seam, pin as before and sew along to the seam. When you get to the part where it joins the next piece take a backstitch, then guide the needle through the seam allowance (so it is loose and not stitched down) and take another backstitch where the next shape starts (E). As you are not sewing into the seam, the panel can be pressed at the end. Note, this is the same method for dealing with seams if you were piecing standard geometric shapes that do not have Y-seams.

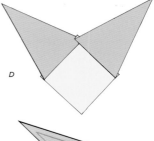

D

E

FINISHING A DESIGN ON-POINT

Placing patches or blocks on point (at a 45-degree angle) can result in them having a very different look. You can also mix them up, with two or more designs put together in this way to result in secondary designs. To find the size of the pieces around the edge you can make a template, but there are also two faster ways of doing this as described here.

Trimming the sides

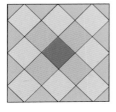

In this method, the patches or blocks are sewn together then the sides cut straight/square at the end. The edge is on the bias when it is cut so it can stretch slightly and so it works best with smaller items, such as when making a block or a piece of patchwork to be used for a cushion.

1 Lay out the patches, then sew them together in diagonal rows (A).

2 Sew the rows together. Pin at the seam intersections as if you were sewing squares in the usual way. The end of each row and the sides of the squares at the corners will overhang the previous piece by ¼in (B). After sewing, carefully give the fabric a good press.

3 Place your panel on your cutting mat. Place your acrylic ruler on top, making sure the edge of the ruler is ¼in (C) away from the points around the edge to allow for seam allowance. When you are happy with the positioning, trim.

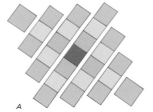

A

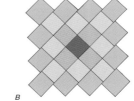

B

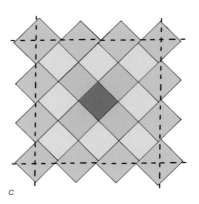

C

Setting Triangles

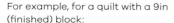

corner triangle

side triangle

These can be used to set square blocks on-point and finish the piece with a straight edge. By following the instructions for how to cut the corner and side setting triangles, you will end up with a straight grain around the edge (or sides).

CALCULATE SIZE OF FABRIC SQUARES

The first thing to do is to calculate the size of the squares that need to be cut into triangles.

FOR CORNER TRIANGLES

These are cut two at a time by cutting a square in half once diagonally. To calculate the size of the square to be cut take the finished block size and divide by 1.414. Round up the number to the nearest ¼in, then add on ⅞in.

For example, for a quilt with a 9in (finished) block:

9 ÷ 1.414 = 6.36, so rounded up this is 6½in

6½in + ⅞in = 7⅜in

FOR SIDE TRIANGLES

These are cut four at a time by cutting a square in half twice diagonally. To calculate the size of the square to be cut take the finished block size and multiply by 1.414. Round up the number to the nearest ¼in, then add on 1¼in.

For example, for a quilt with a 9in (finished) block:

9 x 1.414 = 12.726, so rounded up this is 12¾in

12¾in + 1¼in = 14in

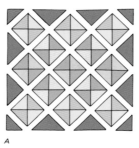

A

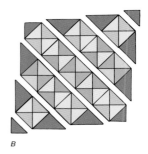

B

ASSEMBLING YOUR QUILT

1 Lay out your blocks into rows, adding side or corner triangles around the edge (A).

2 Sew the blocks into diagonal rows (B), then sew the rows together. When sewing the side triangles, align the straight edge with the side of the block – the point of the triangle will overhang at the other end to allow for the seam allowance after it is stitched and pressed. At the corners, the triangle will be longer at both ends to account for this (see Sewing a Triangle to a Square). Once finished you can trim the edges to neaten, but do make sure there is a ¼in seam allowance all the way around. If your blocks go right to the edge of the design, then make sure you use ¼in seam allowance for your binding, otherwise you will lose the points at the edge.

SEWING A TRIANGLE TO A SQUARE

When a triangle is joined to a square the length of the triangle will always be longer due to the seam allowance. To ensure that once sewn together and the triangle flipped open and pressed, the seams of the triangle and square are aligned, it is important to ensure that the excess fabric at the point of each triangle is even at each end.

A

1 Lay out the triangle next to the square (A). Fold both in half and mark the centre by giving it a press.

2 Place the fabrics right sides together and use the fold mark to line up the centre (B). Place a pin at this point. The ends of the triangle should be longer than the square and there should be an even amount at each end. Sew the seam.

B

3 Trim the excess fabric at the corner of the triangles (C) then open the unit and press the seam (D).

C

D

FOUNDATION PIECING

For this method of sewing patchwork, a paper or fabric foundation is used onto which the design is marked. The fabric pieces are then stitched onto this foundation, working from the back, with the stitching following the marked lines. Sometimes called paper piecing, do not mistake this technique for English paper piecing which is quite different. Machine-sewn foundation piecing is described here.

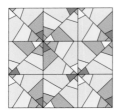 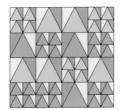

Why Use Foundation Piecing?

Foundation piecing has traditionally been used for string pieced, Log Cabin and miniature quilts, but the main reason modern quilt makers use it so widely is that it helps them to achieve very accurate points, ideal when sewing triangles, for example. It can also be cleverly used to create figurative images, such as animals and flowers.

Types of Paper Foundation

Different papers are suitable as described below. (Note: the paper will be pulled out once the piecing has been completed.)

Standard printer paper Photocopier paper is ideal as you can print the design straight onto it.

Baking paper This is slightly transparent making it easy to see the lines from both sides. The design will need tracing and the paper tears away easily.

Tear-away stabiliser This is transparent and works like baking paper, but it is easier to tear off when finished.

Pre-printed designs These are sold with the design already printed on. The weight can vary, but they are usually similar to standard printer paper.

Foundation Piecing onto Paper

1 Print or trace your design onto paper (A). Cut the paper approximately ½in beyond the dashed outer line (sometimes shown in a lighter colour).

2 Starting with section 1 cut a piece of fabric at least ½in bigger on each side. Place the cut fabric piece on the back of the paper (without the printed lines) over section 1, and hold it up to the light to make sure the edge of the fabric covers the printed or traced lines by at least ¼in (B). Pin it to the paper.

3 Moving on to section 2 cut a piece of fabric at least ½in bigger on each side. Holding it up to the light, check that the edge of the fabric covers the lines by at least ¼in. Carefully flip it so the right side is facing the right side of your first piece (C). To check that the pieces of fabric will cover the lines when sewn, you can test by placing pins along the seam line, opening up the piece of fabric and holding it up to the light to confirm that it not only covers the section but that there is adequate seam allowance. If it needs adjusting remove the pins and move the fabric.

4 When you are happy with the positioning, pin, then sew along the line. The paper side should be facing you with the fabric underneath, so make sure it doesn't flip as it goes under the machine. To secure the stitching, either reverse the stitching at the start and finish, or sew beyond the marked line and into the seam allowance (D). Flip open piece 2, hold it up to the light and double check it covers the lines. Then fold the fabric away from the foundation and trim the seam allowance ¼in away from the line using scissors or a rotary cutting set. Make sure you are only cutting the seam allowance, not the paper or the shape.

5 Flip open the fabric and press using a seam roller or an iron (E). Repeat these steps to add the sections in order until you have completed the design.

6 When the piece is complete, trim on the outer (dashed) line leaving a ¼in seam allowance (F). If you are making lots of units to be joined, sew them together before removing the papers. When removing the papers, if any remain under the stitch lines use tweezers to extract them.

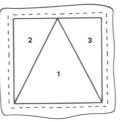

A

— Indicates stitch lines
--- Indicates finished size, plus seam allowance

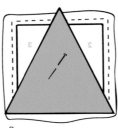

B

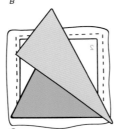

C

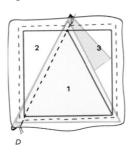

D

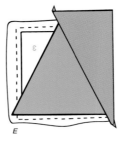

E

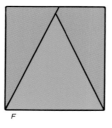

F

Tips for Foundation Piecing

› If you need to attach sheets together for your design, use a glue stick rather than sticky tape as this can leave a sticky residue on the sewing machine needle.

› When starting out, cut the fabric pieces on the generous side. They are easy to trim down, but if not cut big enough you will have to start again.

› Set up your sewing machine with a smaller stitch length (from 1.5 to 2) as this produces a secure stitch and perforates the paper as you sew, making it easier to remove the paper at the end.

› If you have one, place an open-toe foot on your machine as this makes it easy to see and follow the lines.

› When pressing, always use a dry iron but make sure it is not so hot that it scorches the paper.

› When working near the edge of a design, make sure the fabric goes slightly beyond the seam allowance so it can be cut down at the end.

› Be aware of the grain lines when sewing as when the paper is removed the fabric can sometimes distort, especially if working with large pieces. To help ensure the block stays square, only remove the paper once the block has been sewn to the surrounding fabric.

› Sewing through paper blunts the needle so be prepared to change your needle more often. It also creates quite a bit of dust, so clean your machine afterwards.

› If marking your own design, remember to add on the numbers so you know the order in which to sew.

› Foundation piecing can also be sewn by hand. Mark the lines on lightweight fabric or interfacing, then sew the fabric to the foundation using a running stitch. The fabric or interfacing is not removed at the end, so the finished item has an extra layer.

IMPROV PIECING

Improv – short for improvisational – piecing is a technique where patchwork is created using different sizes or shapes of fabric that are sewn together in a less pre-planned and formal way than with traditional piecing. Other names for this technique include free-form and free-piecing, reflecting the informal approach. There are many different methods, but the beauty of this technique is once you get started you can adapt it to make a piece to suit you.

▲ *Detail of the Summer Solstice cushion cover sewn using improv technique.*

Tips for Working with Improv

› Keep an open mind – an improv piece of work usually starts with a rough idea of what you want the finished piece to look like, but evolves as it is made.

› The design can have a regular layout – for example, strips cut in a similar way, joined together and trimmed to the same size – or be completely free-form with panels made in different styles, joined by adding pieces on or trimming down as needed.

› When making lots of pieces of improv using the same technique, for example quarter circles to sew into a quilt, make all the blocks first, then measure the blocks to find the smallest one and trim the rest of the blocks to this size.

› When planning an improv piece, lay out the pieces on a wall or on the floor as you go so you can check that you are happy with the colour/print placement.

› For some of the improv techniques included, such as strips, curves and quarter circles, you can layer two or more pieces of fabric on top of each other before cutting, shuffle the fabrics, then sew to give panels that coordinate with one another.

› Although a ruler is not used to measure when cutting for improv piecing, for safety's sake continue to use one to cut straight lines.

Improv Strips

 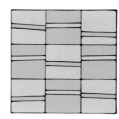

1 Cut your fabric either from a strip or from small pieces leftover from another project. Make sure the angles are random, varying them each time you cut (A).

2 Lay out your pieces so that you end up with a fairly straight piece of patchwork, alternating the angles of your cut strips (B).

3 Sew the pieces together with right sides facing and press, then trim the panel to size to remove any jagged edges (C).

The diagrams show short strips being used but you could use much longer strips too.

A

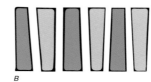

B

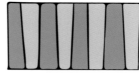

C

Improv Skinny Strips

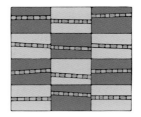 

1 Take a pieced improv strips panel (refer to Improv Strips) and cut a strip from it (A).

2 Take a piece of background fabric and cut once across the middle at a slight angle to give you two background pieces (B).

3 Sew the pieced strip to one of the background pieces, right sides together. Trim the ends level, then sew on the second background piece and trim to size (C).

The diagrams show a pieced strip being inserted into a background fabric, but it can also be made using just one long strip of fabric.

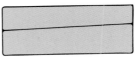

A

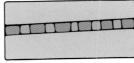

B

C

Sizing for Improv

Improv is usually sewn with a ¼in seam allowance, but due to the nature of the piecing it often requires the fabric to be cut more generously than adding the usual ½in for seam allowance. For example, the top and bottom of a line of strips will end up with a jagged edge due to the varying angles at which they are cut, and so need to be cut slightly longer so the piece can be trimmed straight at the end. Generally, for improv cut your fabric slightly larger than usual, make a sample, then measure to check whether it is just right, or too small, or too large, and adjust as needed. The beauty of this technique is that if it comes up too big you can simply trim it down, and if too small you can just add another piece to it.

Improv Crosses and Kisses

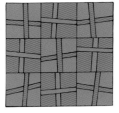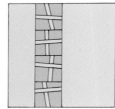

Improv Curves

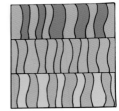

1 Refer to Improv Skinny Strips steps 2 and 3 to insert a skinny strip into a square of background fabric (A).

2 Cut the skinny strip unit in the other direction once across the middle at a slight angle to give you two background pieces. Take another skinny strip and sew it to one of the background pieces, right sides together, then trim the ends level with the background piece (B).

3 With the front of the unit still facing you, take a ruler and line it up with the edge of the short strip and make a small mark on the centre strip, at less than ¼in so it will be hidden in the seam allowance. Repeat on the other side of the strip (C).

4 Take the second piece and place it on top of the first, right sides together. Where the two tiny marks are in the seam allowance of the first piece, match them to the sides of the strip in the second piece. Pin here, and at each end, then sew together (D). Trim to size.

The diagrams show a cross, but place them on the diagonal to make a kiss (or an X).

A

B

make mark either side of centre strip

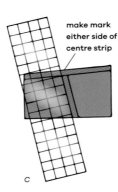

C

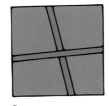

D

1 Lay two pieces of fabric on your cutting mat right sides up. Overlap them enough for the width of the curve. Take your rotary cutter and cut a curve through both layers (A).

2 Take the two pieces and place them next to each other, discarding the other pieces of fabric (B).

3 Place the fabrics right sides together and line them up at the top where you will start sewing. Slowly sew, stopping with the needle down every so often to rearrange the fabric. If you wish to add more fabrics repeat the process. When you have finished, press and trim to size (C).

When cutting the fabrics, make sure they are both right sides up, otherwise you will create a 3D effect. The sharper the angle of the curve, the more technical these are to sew so if you are new to the technique start by cutting a gentle wave.

A

B

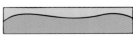

C

Improv Quarter Circles

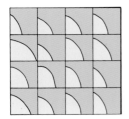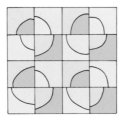

1 Lay two pieces of fabric on your cutting mat right sides up. Overlap them enough for the size of the curve. Take your rotary cutter and cut a curved line through both layers (A).

2 Take the two pieces, one from each fabric, and place them next to each other, saving the other pieces of fabric to make another unit if they are large enough (B).

3 Referring to Curved Piecing: Quarter Circles, sew the pieces together (C); press then trim to size.

4 You can repeat this method to sew more than one curve per unit (D).

A

B

C

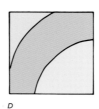

D

When sewing improv curves, it is helpful to mark a line with a fabric-marking tool in the seam across the two pieces of fabric to be joined. Cut the pieces and lay them right side down. Make a small line within the seam allowance. Then when you sew, match up these guide lines.

Improv Log Cabin Block

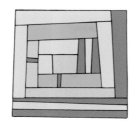

Traditional quilt blocks can be made in an improv way by sewing pieces together without cutting them to an exact size first. The method describes making a Log Cabin design, but this can be adapted to work with triangles and squares too.

1 Take the centre piece (this is improv so it does not need to be a square). Sew a strip onto one side with right sides together. Press open then trim the ends level with the centre – this can be at an angle but it does need to be straight so the next piece can be sewn on (A).

2 Sew another strip onto an adjacent side, repeating the pressing and trimming (B).

3 Repeat step 2 to sew the next strip in place. Remember your strip does not need to be from one piece of fabric – it can be a strip made from several fabrics (refer to Improv Strips and Improv Skinny Strips). Continue adding strips around the centre until the block is the size you want it to be (C).

Cut the pieces larger than required, then trim them down – if you need the block to be a minimum size you can keep adding fabric.

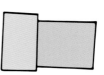
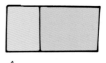

A

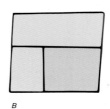

B

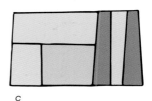

C

APPLIQUÉ

Appliqué is the term for applying one piece of fabric to another. It is often seen with decorative motifs such as leaf or flower shapes and it can be used for adding text to a quilt or putting together an abstract design. As with piecing, there are many different methods of sewing appliqué. The one you choose will depend on which is most suitable for your design, and whether your preference is for hand or machine sewing.

RAW-EDGE APPLIQUÉ

This is a fast way of applying a fabric motif to a background fabric using an adhesive material. With this technique, the edge of the shape applied is not turned under, so if the quilt will require laundering, unless using an extra strong adhesive, or a fabric such as felt that does not fray, you will need to secure your motif with stitch. Repeated washing can reduce the strength of the adhesive, and the raw edges can fray without this.

Materials for Raw-Edge Appliqué

Although fabric adhesive can be used to stick a motif to a background fabric, it can be difficult to apply in a thin and even layer, so paper-backed fusible web is most often used. This is a heat-activated glue backed with paper that gives a smooth finish when an iron is used to fuse it to fabric. It comes in pre-packed sheets or on a roll and different types are available from fabric shops. Always read the manufacturer's instructions before starting, paying particular attention to what temperature to set the iron to and how long to press for.

When working with paper-backed fusible web remember the rough side is the glue side and that you only ever press the smooth (paper) side of the fusible web.

Method for Raw-Edge Appliqué

No seam allowance is required so when preparing the appliqué template cut it to the finished size.

1 Make a template of your appliqué shape (refer to Sewing Basics: Templates). If preparing a motif that cannot be mirrored, such as a number, remember to reverse the template so your motif ends up the correct way around.

2 Cut the fabric for the appliqué approximately ¾in larger than the template, then the paper-backed fusible web about ½in smaller than the fabric (A).

3 Use a fine pencil to lightly draw around the template onto the paper backing (smooth) side of the fusible web (B).

4 Place the appliqué fabric right side down on the ironing board and centre the fusible web, glue (rough) side down, on top. Following the manufacturer's instructions, press (C). As the web has been cut slightly smaller than the fabric it should not melt onto your ironing board.

5 Use scissors to cut out the appliqué shape following the drawn line (D), then peel off the paper backing. If the backing does not come away easily, carefully score it with a pin.

6 Place the backing fabric on the ironing board right side facing up and position the appliqué shape onto it, also right side facing up and press to fuse in place (E).

7 Finish the edge of the appliqué shape with hand or machine stitching of your choosing if desired.

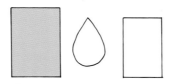

A

B

C

cut

D

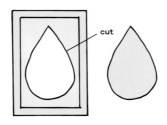

E

Tips for Working with Raw-Edge Appliqué

› If you find the paper-backed fusible web leaves too firm a finish, cut out the centre of the web leaving an outer border of about ½in. This means only the outer part of the design is fused.

› Press using an up and down motion: never iron from side to side as it can distort the motif.

› Place a piece of baking paper on your ironing board and another on top of your fabric to protect it from any stray glue that can melt out from the edges.

› If stitching around the edges of your appliqué motif, choose your thread colour carefully, selecting a toning colour for 'invisible' stitching or a contrast colour for added interest.

› Store any small fabric offcuts backed with fusible web in a box as they come in useful when making smaller projects, such as cards and mini quilts.

› When appliquéing a paler fabric to a darker one, the background can shadow through. To prevent this, you can fuse a piece of white fabric to the back of the motif first, to make it more opaque.

› You don't always have to draw around a template – for a more organic shape, cut freehand with scissors.

HAND SEWING RAW-EDGE APPLIQUÉ

There are many different ways to hand stitch the motif to the background fabric to make it more durable and several are listed below. Refer to Sewing Basics: Hand Sewing Stitches for more detail.

Whip stitch Oversew the edges with short straight stitches for a neat finish (A): experiment with changing the stitch length, placing them further apart or closer together.

Blanket stitch This has the effect of framing the motif (B): try to make sure the line of stitching is next to (not on) the outline of the shape.

Embroidery stitches Different stitches, such as cross stitches worked over the edge (C), or a running stitch worked close to the edge, can look interesting.

A

B

C

MACHINE SEWING RAW-EDGE APPLIQUÉ

You may prefer to machine stitch your appliqué motif to the background fabric and, if so, it is a good idea to place a sheet of tear-away stabiliser behind the background fabric to prevent puckering. Alternatively, you can layer up the quilt – backing, wadding (batting) and quilt top – then machine sew around the motifs through all three layers. Some options for machine sewing include:

Straight stitch Work the line of stitching slightly in from the motif edge (A). When washed several times, the edge will fray up to the stitched line for a soft-looking finish.

Zigzag stitch Try out different widths and lengths to find a stitch to suit (B). To cover the fabric edge completely, use a very narrow width for a satin stitch effect.

Free-motion stitching Using a darning foot, you can draw around the motif with free-motion stitching; do this several times for a pencil sketch effect (C).

A

B

C

When machine sewing, pull the bobbin thread through to the front when you start, then when you have finished use a hand sewing needle to take the threads to the back to tie them off.

◀ *A detail of zigzag stitch being used to edge circle motifs.*

TURNED EDGE APPLIQUÉ

With turned edge appliqué techniques there are no raw edges to deal with and so fraying is not an issue. It is suitable for all types of shapes and motifs can be layered on top of one another. These techniques are usually hand sewn, but if you turn the edges beforehand as with the pre-turning a hem method, it is possible to machine sew motifs onto the background.

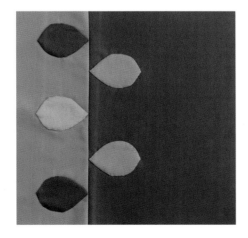

When pressing a finished piece of turned edge appliqué press from the back using a pressing cloth to avoid flattening the design.

Turn-As-You-Go

With this method you draw the outer line of the design on the front of the fabric, then hand stitch along this line, folding a hem under as you go.

1 Make a template of your appliqué shape out of card or template plastic (refer to Sewing Basics: Templates); do not add on seam allowance.

2 Place your template on top of the right side of the appliqué fabric and draw around it using a removable fabric pen or pencil. Cut the fabric out a scant ¼in away from the line (A).

3 Pin the appliqué motif onto the backing fabric (B).

4 Start sewing in the middle of an edge if possible (not at a corner or tight curve). At your start point, use the drawn line as a guide and fold under the excess fabric for about 1in and finger press. Then slip stitch along this fold (C) to sew the motif to the backing fabric. Stop every so often to fold and finger press the fabric so you have a neat hem to sew. If needed, clip or notch any points or curves as you go (refer to Dealing with Points and Curves).

A

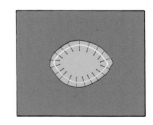

B

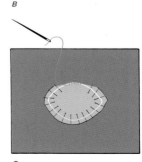

C

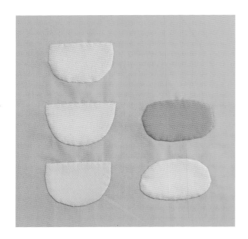

Pre-Turning a Hem

With this method, paper, thin card or freezer paper is used to create a resist to fold the fabric to make a hem, which means you do not have to turn the fabric as you go. If making a quilt with lots of motifs, you can prepare them in advance and store in a tin until you are ready to sew.

1 Draw around the template onto thin card or the matt side of the freezer paper using a pencil (do not add seam allowance), then cut out on the marked line.

2 Take a piece of fabric for the appliqué and place it right side down on an ironing board. Place the template on top of the appliqué fabric, making sure there is at least ¼in excess fabric all around. Use a fabric glue stick to temporarily hold the card in place; if using freezer paper, place it shiny side down, and press with a dry iron to fix it to the fabric. Cut out the fabric shape a scant ¼in away from the template. If required, clip or notch any points or curves into the seam allowance around the edge of the fabric (refer to Dealing with Points and Curves).

3 Carefully fold the seam allowance over the freezer paper template and press to hold, choosing one of the following methods:

Method 1 Fold the seam allowance over the paper, thin card or freezer paper and press (to make sure it holds its shape, use a cotton bud to place a small amount of starch under the seam allowance before pressing).

Method 2 Fold and tack (baste) the seam allowance into place as if you were preparing shapes for English paper piecing (see Piecing: English Paper Piecing). Remove this tacking (basting) when you need to remove the paper, thin card or freezer paper.

Method 3 Use a fabric glue stick to hold the hem in place.

APPLYING THE MOTIF TO A BACKGROUND

The background fabric can sometimes pull in and shrink slightly as the appliqué is sewn, and the edges can fray if you are handling it a lot. It is a good idea, therefore, to cut the background fabric larger than required and trim it down to size once the design has been applied. Use your ruler as a guide to ensure the motif is placed where you want it, or draw the design onto a piece of tracing paper or thin interfacing and place this on top of the background fabric to help with positioning the motifs.

SECURING MOTIF TO BACKGROUND FABRIC

First secure the turned edge appliqué motif in place on the background fabric. You could use a fabric glue stick to hold it in place temporarily, but using appliqué pins is a more secure option (A). These are shorter than standard pins which means thread is less likely to get tangled around them when you are sewing, and their size means more can be placed through the motif.

HAND STITCHING TO BACKGROUND FABRIC

Using a toning thread for invisible stitches, slip stitch to sew around the edge of the appliqué motif. If you prefer you can remove the template from the back of the motif before sewing it to the background fabric, and this is a particularly good option if you need to sew into the motif where there are sharp points. Alternatively, you can leave it in while you are hand sewing the motif to the backing. Once stitching is complete, take a pair of small scissors to carefully cut a small incision in the backing fabric, making sure you do not cut through to the front of the appliqué motif or too close to the sewn edge. Remove the template through this hole (B). Or, if you prefer you can cut away the backing fabric to ¼in inside the edge of the appliqué shape (C). This leaves one layer and helps prevent a darker background fabric shadowing through.

MACHINE STITCHING TO BACKGROUND FABRIC

To machine stitch the appliqué motif, the template must be removed, then it can be carefully machine sewn onto the background fabric. Take extra care at corners and points, and you may want to use a fabric glue stick to adhere it to the background first.

If working on appliqué motifs that will be layered, you do not need to prepare the edges where a shape will be covered by another.

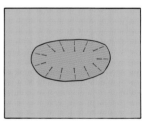

A

B

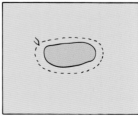

C

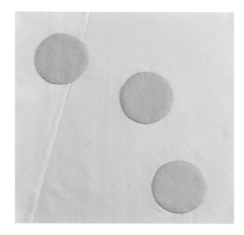

Circle Appliqué

Circles make a pleasing design in appliqué and are fairly simple to prepare. Start by making a circle template using a template, a compass, or by trying out different items in your kitchen, from cups to plates, to find one that is the right size.

1 Make a circle template of your finished size using card or the type of template plastic that does not melt. Draw around the circle template onto the wrong side of your appliqué fabric (A). Cut the fabric ½in bigger all the way around to allow for the seam allowance.

2 Tack (baste) all the way around the edge, using a doubled (or strong) thread, in between the drawn circle and raw edge of the fabric (B).

3 Place the template in the centre of the fabric, aligning the edge with the drawn circle. Gently pull on the tacking (basting) thread to gather the fabric around the template and press around the edge (a spray of starch can help to keep its shape) (C). Smooth any pointy edges with your fingers for a smooth circle and press well to hold the hem around the edge in place.

4 Once the fabric is cool, carefully remove the template. (It is not necessary to remove the tacking (basting) stitches unless you wish to as they are on the back so won't be seen.)

5 Give the circle a press from the front to make sure the edge is flat (D). Appliqué to a background fabric with an invisible hand slip stitch, as in the stitched sample, or by machine.

A

B

C

D

Dealing with Points and Curves

To achieve a neat finish, the appliqué shapes may need some extra preparation in certain areas, such as at sharp points. If you need to manipulate the fabric into a certain place, give it a finger press or use a seam roller or iron (a mini iron is perfect) to get the fabric to go where you need it to.

POINTS

Inside points Clip into the seam allowance, stopping a few threads short of the drawn line (A). When sewing the shape to the background, make a stitch at this point to prevent fraying.

Outside points Trim the seam allowance to reduce bulk, then fold the seam allowance from one direction, then the other, to neatly tuck it behind the motif (B).

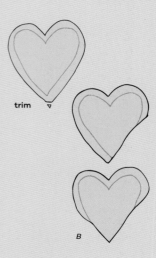

For hand sewing appliqué use a finer thread to give a more invisible finish.

CURVES

Inside (concave) curves If there is bulk, clip straight snips into the seam allowance about every ¼in to enable the fabric to be smoothly turned (A).

Outside (convex) curves If there is bulk, cut tiny V shapes in the seam allowance, so that there is less fabric to be turned under (B). Take small stitches to ensure a smooth curve.

A

B

OTHER APPLIQUÉ METHODS

As with piecing, there are a wide range of appliqué methods, so there will usually be a technique which lends itself to your quilt design. Reverse appliqué is a technique which can get you starting to think about negative space and can be combined with other techniques such as using a background made from a piece of improv. Bias strip appliqué is a handy technique to have in your toolkit if you like designing with graphic shapes.

Reverse Appliqué

In this method of appliqué two layers of fabric (sometimes more) are placed together, then the motif is cut out of the front fabric to reveal the fabric layer(s) beneath. The method described turns the fabric and hand sews the hem, but it can also be done with a raw edge that is machine sewn to secure and prevent it fraying.

1 Select the fabric for the front layer and use your template (that doesn't include seam allowance) to draw the motif onto it.

2 Place the fabric on top of the second layer of fabric and pin or tack (baste) around the edge to hold the fabric layers together (A). Using a small, sharp pair of scissors, carefully cut the fabric away in the middle of the motif to within about ¼in from the drawn line (B).

3 If necessary, clip or notch any points or curves (refer to Turned Edge Appliqué: Dealing with Points and Curves). Then using the marked line as a guide, fold under the seam working on about a 2in section at a time and sew in place using slip stitch (see Turned Edge Appliqué: Turn-As-You-Go) (C). At the end, if you wish, carefully cut away the excess fabric on the back at least ¼in away from the sewn line.

For small or intricate motifs, trim the seam allowance narrower than ¼in so the hem lays flatter.

A

B

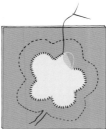

C

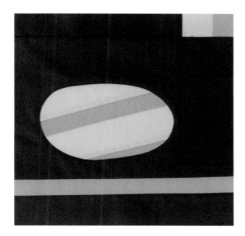

Prepared Edge Reverse Appliqué

In this method of appliqué, the shape is cut out of the top layer fabric and the edges turned to create a hem, then it is applied onto the background fabric. This creates the effect of the background fabric being placed in a frame. Rounded shapes are best, although more intricate shapes can work as long as the points are prepared (refer to Turned Edge Appliqué).

1 Cut a piece of freezer paper 2in larger all round than your finished design. For example, for a 4 x 10in oval, cut the freezer paper 6 x 12in. Working on the matt side of the paper, trace your template in the centre (A) and cut out the shape.

A

2 Place the freezer paper shiny side down onto the wrong side of your top layer fabric where you want the motif to go, and press to adhere. Cut away the fabric behind the gap in the centre of the freezer paper allowing for a turning hem of approximately ⅜in of excess fabric (B).

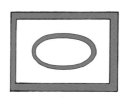

B

3 Clip into the excess fabric at regular intervals, then apply starch to the seam allowance using a cotton bud or paintbrush. Fold the hem to the back and press, working your way all around the shape (C). When it has cooled, remove the freezer paper.

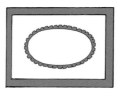

C

4 With right sides facing up, place the prepared front panel on top of the background fabric, which needs to be at least 1in larger than the cut-out shape. Pin or tack (baste) to hold the layers together, then slip stitch around the hemmed shape to the back or carefully machine sew about ⅛in in from the hem. Turn to the wrong side and cut away the excess backing fabric about ⅜in away from the sewn line (D).

D

Bias Strip Appliqué

These strips are versatile for appliqué and can be used straight or curved. The easiest way to make bias strips of an identical width is with bias bars. Bias bars are either made from metal or from a type of plastic that does not melt when placed inside a sewn strip of fabric and ironed. Note, this method does not require the fabric strip to be turned as the seam is hidden on the back.

Sizing notes Measure the width of the bar, multiply this by two, add on ½in for seam allowance, then ⅛in for ease. Make a small sample strip to ensure it fits; if it does not then adjust the measurement accordingly.

1 Cut your strips of fabric on the bias (i.e., at a 45-degree angle to the weave). If you need a longer strip, then sew strips together using a 45-degree seam (refer to Binding: Joining Strips Together). Take a strip and fold it in half, wrong sides together, and sew the long edge using a ¼in seam allowance (A).

2 Trim the seam allowance to ⅛in (B).

3 Place the bias bar in the strip and turn the seam so it is in the middle of the bar, or slightly to one side. Press the strip, making sure the seam allowance is behind the strip (C). If you are working on a long strip, start at one end and press, then slide the bar up and press again, and so on. Remove the bias bar.

4 The finished bias strip (D) is now ready to be sewn in place. This can be done with an invisible hand slip stitch, or machine sewn along each edge.

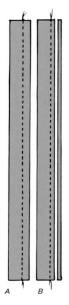

A *B*

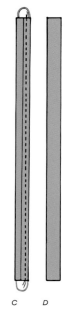

C *D*

FINISHING

Patchwork needs to go through several processes to become a finished quilt, and these are covered in this chapter. Firstly, it needs to be joined together, then the top, wadding (batting) and backing need layering. Next comes quilting. This opens a world of design possibilities, as the way in which the layers are stitched can radically alter the personality of the quilt. This can be done by hand or machine, depending on personal preference. Finally, the edges of the quilt are completed with binding so the piece is durable and ready to be used.

LAYERING A QUILT

Quilts are made from three layers – the quilt top, the backing fabric and the filling in between, which is usually wadding (batting). Wadding gives a quilt warmth and adds texture, although if you want to make a lightweight quilt you can choose to use another layer of fabric in the middle. Alternatively, you can make a coverlet, which is just two layers – the top and a backing.

Assembling a Quilt Top

It may be that your quilt is put together as you go, for example square blocks joined together in the same way as smaller squares, or improv panels of different sizes joined together with the help of the partial seam technique. However, if you are using sashing (strips that go between blocks) or adding a border (a frame around the edge) you will need to cut strips. These can be worked out by calculating the size that the blocks or the quilt should end up according to the units sewn. Sometimes despite best efforts, quilts can vary slightly in size from one side to the other, especially when they are large. If you are adding a border or cutting binding and the size seems slightly out, the best way to get the actual width is to measure each side, then at least once across the centre. Add these together, then divide by how many measurements you have taken to get an average (so if you have taken three then divide by three), then make this strip to fit the quilt. Repeat to calculate the length, then cut your strips to this size (see Piecing: Squares and Strips – Tips for Working with Strips).

Once the top is assembled, the next task is to give it a good press and remove any stray threads and tidy up any frayed seams. This is particularly important if working with high contrast fabrics as a slight fray in the seam allowance of a dark fabric could shadow and be seen behind the paler fabric it is next to.

Choosing a Backing Fabric

The fabric you choose for the back layer of your quilt will often depend on what it will be used for. If it requires drape, for laying on a bed for example, you'll want to choose a fabric that is the same weight as the front. If you are making a wall hanging, then you may want to consider a heavier weight fabric. The main issue tends to be finding fabric that is wide enough, so look out for extra-wide fabric in quilt shops; these can be as much as 108in wide. If you need to join fabric together to make the backing, then use a ½in seam allowance, and press the seams open so that the bulk created by the seam cannot be seen on the front of the quilt. To disguise a seam when joining two pieces of printed fabric, fold in a hem on one piece, lay it over the other and move it until the print is aligned, then pin and sew along the crease. A pieced back made from two or more fabrics can look interesting, and you could incorporate a spare sample or block into the backing.

SIZING

Your backing fabric and wadding (batting) need to be bigger than the quilt top, generally at least 2in wider each side, but this goes up to 4in for larger quilts, or if you are using a long-arm quilt service. The wadding and backing may pull in slightly during the quilting process, and cutting these larger also means you don't have to worry about getting them exactly aligned when layering.

Types of Wadding (Batting)

There are many types of wadding (batting) available, including wool, cotton, bamboo, and blends such as cotton and polyester mix – there is even one available made from plastic bottles. General rules for fibres apply to waddings, so natural fibres such as wool and cotton tend to be more breathable, while polyester usually stands up well to repeated washing. Cotton and bamboo tend to be easier to machine quilt than hand quilt, while polyester is preferred by hand quilters. Prices can vary with polyester wadding being considerably cheaper than wool or silk.

Some terms you may come across when selecting wadding include:

Shrinkage Most waddings will shrink by a small percentage when first washed, and this is noted on the packaging. The shrinkage gives the quilt a textured look, but if you do not want this, then carefully pre-wash the wadding before quilting.

Needle-punched, scrim and bonded These are terms for different mechanical processes that the fibres go through to create wadding (batting).

Drape This refers to how a wadding looks when you hold it up. Softer waddings will tend to have more drape and so be suitable for sofa quilts, while stiffer waddings are better for wall hangings.

Loft This generally refers to the thickness. High loft will mean that the quilting (where the layers are held together) will have more definition than on a low loft wadding, which will be quite flat.

Colour Most waddings are unbleached so they are a light cream colour, although bleached white for light quilts and black for dark quilts are also available. Sometimes the wadding can shadow through behind the fabric, so choose one to suit your fabric choices.

Insulated This is a special wadding suitable for making items that may come into contact with heat, such as oven gloves or pot holders.

Some companies sell wadding (batting) sample packs so you can feel them for yourself and try sewing through them and laundering them to see how they wash before purchasing a large piece.

PREPARING WADDING (BATTING)

Always check the wadding (batting) instructions to see how far apart the stitches need to be. If you only need a stitch every 8in then you can do less quilting, if every 2in, then you will need to do more. It is important to quilt as recommended as if you don't, then the wadding could eventually disintegrate and ball up. If you buy pre-packed wadding, open it before layering and place on a bed for a day to help remove the creases. Some quilters like to press wadding but this will depend on the fibre used and whether it can be pressed. Care must be taken as pressing can flatten the wadding and so decrease the loft, although this may be the look you want to achieve.

The Process of Layering

The purpose of the layering stage is to hold the layers of your quilt together ready for quilting. It is quite straightforward to do but increases in difficulty as the size of the quilt top you are working on gets bigger.

LAYERING

1 Lay your pressed backing on a table or the floor wrong side up. If needed, you can place low-tack masking tape around the edges of the fabric to hold it flat but don't pull the fabric too taut (A).

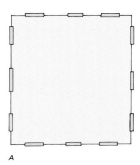

A

2 Gently place your wadding (batting) on top of the backing fabric. Smooth the wadding from the middle to the outside edges so that it lays flat and there are no creases (B).

B

3 Place your quilt top right side up in the middle of the wadding. Smooth your quilt top until it is flat across the layers (C).

4 Once you are happy that all the quilt layers are flat, temporarily fasten them together using one of the joining methods (see Joining the Layers). Work methodically in a grid format, from the centre out towards the edge of the quilt top.

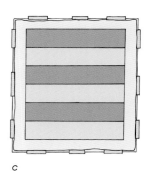

C

JOINING THE LAYERS

The layered quilt, sometimes referred to as a quilt sandwich, must be temporarily secured at regular intervals to prevent the layers moving during quilting and this can be done in various ways:

Pins Using quilter's safety pins (those with a slight curve are best), start in the middle and pin through the layers every 4in (A). This technique is mainly used for machine quilting as you can remove a pin just before you quilt in that area.

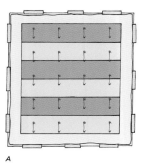

A

Tacking (basting) Using thread and a darning needle, stitch lines of long tacking (basting) stitch from the centre out towards the edge of the quilt (B). This technique is mainly used for hand quilting when the fabric is placed in a frame.

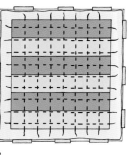

B

Spray adhesive This is a glue that is applied *between* the layers. To use, lay out the backing fabric, place the wadding (batting) on top and smooth, then fold half the wadding back and lightly spray the backing fabric, before placing the wadding back on top. Repeat with the other half. Attach the quilt top to the wadding in the same way. Read the manufacturer's instructions before beginning and use in a well-ventilated room (or wear a mask). Always clean the nozzle after use to prevent jamming which can result in uneven application.

QUILTING

Quilting is simply the process that holds the layers of a quilt together and can be sewn by hand or machine. There are lots of choices to be made, such as what method and thread colour to use. At one end of the spectrum, the quilt design can be the main focus of a piece, adding texture and pattern to cloth, and at the other it can be minimal and purely functional to turn the piece of patchwork into a quilt.

Marking Quilting Lines

There are times you will not need to mark a design, for example, using the edge of the sewing machine foot to follow a seam line, but when you do need to mark up the quilt top, test your chosen tool on a scrap of fabric before starting to make sure it can be removed. A design can be marked either before or after layering. If doing it before, be aware that some markers, such as chalk, can brush off during the layering process. Your options include:

Pens Water-soluble pen lines can be removed by dabbing with a wet kitchen towel but only completely disappear when your project is washed. Air-erasable pen lines fade and how long this takes will depend on climate, so check they remain in place long enough to sew. If ironed both water-soluble and air-erasable pen lines will fix and be impossible to remove. They are available with different sized nibs for thick or fine lines.

Chalk (or dressmaker's) pencil Available in different colours, this is designed to wash-out. Keep a pencil sharpener handy to make sure of a sharp, accurate line. If you need a fine line, then a fabric propelling pencil is recommended.

Chalk Tailor's chalk is handy, but the line can be thick. A good alternative is a chalk wheel, which releases a fine line of chalk.

Quilter's masking tape This is ideal for marking straight lines, for example when cross-hatch quilting. Quilt close to the edge of the tape, never on top of it, as it can then be difficult to remove; do not leave on fabric for more than a day or the sticky residue may be transferred.

Pressure marker This works by applying pressure to create a line that can be followed. Clover's Hera marker is popular with quilters as it gives a fine line and won't damage the quilt top.

Quilting Design Decisions

You may have decided on a quilting pattern at the beginning of the project and so you can dive straight in to the quilting process. Alternatively, if you have been focused on making the top, you may now be pausing to consider your options for how you want the finished piece to look. Some of the choices for a quilt design include:

Echo This is where you follow the edge of the patchwork or motif, for example stitching around a triangle.

Allover This is where the quilting ignores the shapes created by the piecing of the quilt.

In the ditch This is where the quilting is hidden in the seam line.

Fabric inspired This is where inspiration is taken from the fabric print, for example quilting circles if one of the fabrics has circles on it.

It can be a good idea to try drawing the quilting design onto an image of the quilt to see how it will look and to work through some different ideas before starting. This can be tracing paper placed on top of a printed image or by using software to draw directly onto a photo.

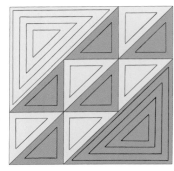
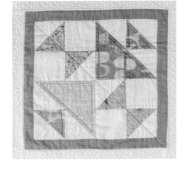

Echo

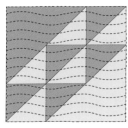
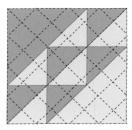
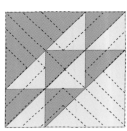
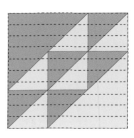
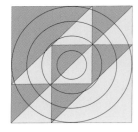
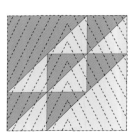

Allover

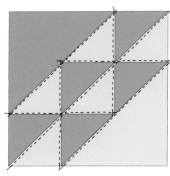
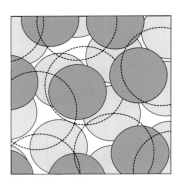

In the ditch

Fabric inspired

Tips for Quilting

› When planning the design, consider how you will be using your quilt. Less quilting gives a softer drape while intense close-up machine quilting can make the finished piece firm, which is ideal for wall hangings but not so good for bed quilts.

› Don't be afraid to mix and match quilting methods. For example, a quilt could have straight line machine quilting across it, then big stitch hand quilting added in specific areas using a contrast thread.

› Whether quilting by hand or machine, start in the centre (or at one side) and work out to the edges so you are smoothing out the layers all the time so they stay nice and flat.

Hand Quilting

Hand quilting is usually done with a type of running stitch sewn across the quilt. It can be a very small stitch using fine thread with a betweens needle, or big stitches using thicker thread, such as cotton perle size 8 or 12, with a chenille or embroidery needle.

▲ *These lines were marked with tape, then sewn using a chenile 22 needle and size 8 perle thread.*

QUILTING WITHOUT A FRAME

It is easy to quilt without a frame, although it is important to make sure the quilt is kept flat (by placing it on a table, for example) and regularly smoothed.

1 Start by securing the thread end in the layers. Make a quilter's knot (refer to Sewing Basics) and, with the front of the quilt facing you and at least 1in away from where you want to begin quilting, take the needle through the quilt top and wadding (batting) layers only (but not through the backing) and bring it up to the front at the point where you want to start quilting (A).

2 Gently pull the needle so the knot pops though the layers and pull on the thread to secure the knot in the wadding. If the knot resists, it may be too big to comfortably go through the weave of the fabric, and if it easily goes all the way through, it is not big enough: if either proves to be the case, cut the knot off and make another one to suit the fabric. Trim the excess thread (B)

3 One stitch length from your start point, insert your needle through all layers to begin your running stitch line. Ideally, try to take it through at as near a 90-degree angle (so perpendicular to the quilt) as possible (C). Taking the needle to the back, travel along and come back up to the front (D). Pull the thread through and you have made your first stitch.

4 Continue in this way; once you are in a rhythm you may want to load more stitches onto the needle before pulling it through (E).

5 To finish, stop before you run out of thread. Make a knot in the end against the quilt top (F), then take the needle back through the quilt top at the exit point of your last stitch, travel a little way through the wadding, pulling the knot through to secure it in the layers, then bring the needle back out and trim the excess thread.

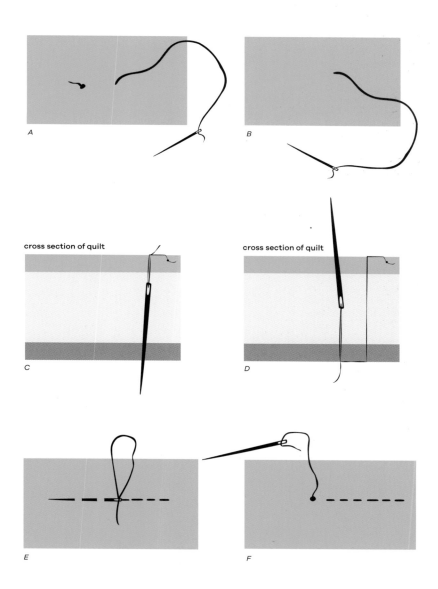

cross section of quilt

cross section of quilt

A

B

C

D

E

F

QUILTING USING A FRAME

A frame keeps the layers smooth while you quilt. There are different types available including hoops, snap frames and free-standing frames. The technique below describes the traditional rocking technique where the end of your finger creates the running stitch but it is also possible to sew a normal quick running stitch (where you hold the needle between your thumb and forefinger) in a frame, if the tension is loose enough.

1 Place your quilt in the frame making sure it is not too tight as if there is no 'give' you won't be able to manipulate it to stitch. You'll need both hands free, so unless you are using a free-standing frame, rest your frame against a table. Referring to Quilting Without a Frame, steps 1 and 2, secure your thread. Place a thimble on the end of the second or third fingers of both hands. One hand will be on top of the quilt, the other on the bottom. One stitch length away from where you started, insert the needle through the layers at a 90-degree angle using the thimble on top (A). This should meet with the thimble underneath which pushes upwards and so makes sure the needle has gone all the way through to the back.

2 Place the thumb of the hand on top into the fabric ahead of where you will be stitching. With the thimble underneath pushing up, this creates a raised area to take the needle through. Then use the thimble at the end of the needle to push the needle along (B) and come back out on top to make a small stitch. Repeat, loading more stitches onto your needle. If you are new to this method, take one stitch at a time whilst you get used to positioning your hands.

3 Continue to quilt in this way, making sure the needle goes through all the layers. Finish the stitching referring to Quilting Without a Frame, step 5.

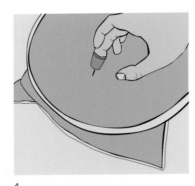

A

B

Snap frames, which pack down into a small space, are easy to use – just twist the sides to adjust the tension.

DECORATIVE STITCHES

Running stitch is an easy hand quilting stitch, creating an even line that looks similar on both quilt front and back. You can experiment with it, of course, by making the stitches different lengths (A, B). This works best with thicker thread and for guidance you can buy a special tape that has lines marked on it which you can sew alongside to make sure the stitches are the length you want them to be. If you want to experiment with other stitches such as cross stitch (C), then as long as they are no more than 1in apart, you can travel the thread through the layers between stitches. Seed stitches can also look effective for building up an area of texture (D).

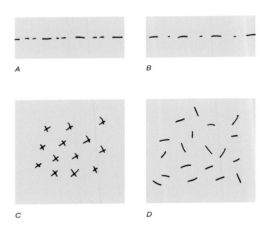

A

B

C

D

Tips for Hand Quilting

› When starting hide the knot and tail in the wadding (batting) along the direction in which you will be sewing as this means you will be quilting over the tail of the thread and thus making it extra secure.

› For a long line of quilting, start in the middle with a length of thread, then work one way and then the other.

› If you want to make sure the thread is really secure, take a backstitch at the start and finish, but if using a thicker thread on a paler fabric these additional stitches may stand out.

› Relax and enjoy the process of hand quilting. Do not worry too much about even sized stitches; the more you do, the easier it gets.

Machine Quilting

This is a quick way to quilt and gives a strong finish and so is very suitable for quilts that will be machine washed and tumble dried. You can create straight or curved lines and so there are endless design possibilities.

PREPARING YOUR MACHINE

Read the section on threads (see Tools and Equipment) and machine sewing needles (see Sewing Basics) before starting. As you are sewing through three layers a little preparation is needed to ensure the layers do not shift and pucker. If working on a smaller project, such as a cushion, you can use a standard foot and reduce the foot pressure (check your sewing machine manual), but for a larger project a walking foot (also called a dual feed foot) is essential. The foot contains feed dogs which work with those on your machine to guide the layers through evenly without pushing or puckering them. Some machines have a walking foot built in. You will also need to alter the stitch length. As the stitches are going through multiple layers they are usually set to a longer stitch than for piecing, and this will be at least a 3, more depending on your preference.

PREPARING YOURSELF

When machine quilting, remember to have good posture. It can be put a lot of strain on your shoulders and neck, so sit up straight and have regular breaks. If working on a large quilt, make sure it is supported by a table or chair. This helps to keep the stitching even and protects your wrists and shoulders. You can also buy quilting gloves that have small grips and so make it easier for your hands to move the fabric.

▲ *Detail of straight line machine quilting.*

STRAIGHT LINE MACHINE QUILTING

This method of quilting uses the straight stitch on your sewing machine. However, it can also be used for waves and curves, so it has lots of possibilities.

1 Start your stitching with both the top and bobbin thread at the front of your work. This eliminates the risk of the bobbin thread tangling on the back of the quilt. To do this, place the quilt under the presser foot where you want to begin quilting and hold on to the top thread. Lower and raise the needle then lightly pull on the top thread. This should bring the bobbin thread through to the front. (This is exactly the same as what you do to bring up the bobbin thread when you start sewing, but here you are taking it through the layers.)

2 Place both threads to the back of the foot and secure the stitching using one of the methods described in Securing the Threads at the Start and Finish and start quilting.

3 Use your hands to gently ease the fabric where you want it to go. Do not pull it, and make sure the weight of the quilt is supported either on a table next to the machine or on a chair. If you need to change the direction of your quilting, or to readjust at any time, stop with the needle down through the fabric, lift the presser foot and pivot the fabric. Then, when you start quilting again, it will be from exactly the same spot.

▲ *A walking foot and clear open-toe free-motion foot.*

SECURING THE THREADS AT THE START AND FINISH

Here are four different ways to secure the threads when machine quilting. Once the thread is secure the ends can be trimmed so it looks the same on the back and the front.

SECURE WITH SMALL STITCHES

Set the stitch length to its shortest setting. Take about five stitches, then stop. Put the stitch length up to the size you are using, then start quilting. When you want to stop quilting repeat the process.

SECURE WITH A BACKSTITCH

Use the reverse function on your sewing machine to secure the thread. It is quick but the downside of this technique is it can leave a thicker line of stitching where you have begun or finished, so it works best with thread and fabric that are the same colour.

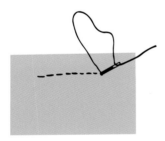

TYING OFF THREADS

When you have finished quilting, use a hand sewing needle to take the threads through to the back of the quilt. Tie them together in a knot, then use a hand sewing needle to hide the ends in the wadding (batting). Cut off any excess thread. If you are hiding them near a quilting line, you can take the needle under the line so that they are especially secure. Secure and invisible, this method is the most time consuming!

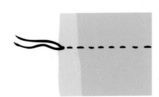

NO SECURING

Start and finish quilting in the wadding (batting) at the very edge of the quilt. The ends will be secured when the binding is attached to the quilt. To stop the tail ends getting caught, trim them to about 2in after each line of quilting has been completed.

If sewing lines from one side to the other, start the quilting on alternate sides each time. If you always start from the same side it could distort your quilt.

FREE-MOTION QUILTING

With this method of quilting you are moving the fabric rather than the foot feeding the quilt under the machine. It is great for creating designs with curves and swirls and, in addition to quilting, it can be used to 'draw' around appliqué motifs. If you are new to this, or returning after a break, practise on some smaller samples, as this helps to warm up your eye/hand coordination. Try to relax and, to focus on your stitching, remove any distractions – set your phone to silent and put some music on. If you want a more controlled result you can buy specially designed free-motion rulers to use as a guide, or draw your design onto a thin piece of paper (such as a tear-away stabiliser), place this on top of the fabric, follow the lines as you stitch, then remove it at the end.

PREPARING YOUR MACHINE

Read the section on threads (see Tools and Equipment) and machine sewing needles (see Sewing Basics) before starting. Fit a darning foot to your machine. There are different types available: an clear open-toe one is a good option for quilting as you can see exactly where the stitches are being formed, but any darning foot is suitable. Set the stitch length to 0 and drop or cover the feed dogs (refer to your sewing machine manual for advice). If you have one, use an extension (or drop-in) table that puts your machine at the same level as your work surface, as this will make it easier to move the fabric (you can also fit a sliding mat onto the machine).

1 To start sewing bring both threads up to the front and place them towards the back of the machine

2 Take a few stitches on the spot to secure the thread, then start sewing, carefully moving the fabric. As you are moving the fabric under the needle, the size of the stitches made will depend on how fast your machine is going versus how fast you are moving the fabric. If the thread tails get in the way, stop with the needle through the fabric and trim them off.

3 When you want to finish your stitching take a few stitches on the spot to secure, remove the quilt from the machine and trim any excess threads

BINDING

Once quilting is completed the edges need neatening with binding. There are different ways of doing this, and each has its own characteristics as described below, but all of them neaten the edge of the quilt and make it durable for use. If possible, use a walking foot for sewing binding as this will help to feed your project evenly through the machine, as there can be up to five layers being sewn.

Preparing a Quilt for Binding

Before sewing the binding, the excess wadding (batting) and backing need trimming level with the quilt top. To do this, use your rotary cutting set, and make sure the corners are square before cutting. It can be helpful to sew all around the very edge of the quilt (so it will be hidden by the binding) using a long machine stitch to hold the layers together; this will prevent the layers from shifting when you are sewing on the binding.

▲ Binding detail from the Night Sky Quilt of single-fold binding with straight corners.

Preparing Single-Fold and Double-Fold Binding

This type of binding adds a border of fabric around the edge of the quilt. You can use one layer of fabric (single-fold) or two layers (double-fold). The strips can be sewn to create square corners, or mitred. When choosing your fabric think about whether you want it to contrast and act like a frame, or to be subtle and fade into the finished design. You can also join together leftover fabric from the piecing stage or use a different fabric along each edge.

Binding can vary in width, and this will depend on the width of the strips cut and seam allowance used. The measurements provided are for a ¼in wide binding for where blocks go right to the edge of the quilt, and a ⅜in wide binding which can give a bolder look.

The aim is to have the binding roughly the same width on the back and the front, and for the folded edge of the binding to cover the line of machine stitching. Things such as the thickness of the wadding (batting) can affect this, so sew a few inches of binding at the beginning and take it from the machine to check you are happy with the widths. If not, adjust your seam allowance accordingly.

The methods described can be mixed, so single-fold binding can be sewn with mitred corners and double-fold binding with straight corners.

JOINING STRIPS TOGETHER

Strips are usually cut along the length or width of the fabric (they only need to be cut on the bias if the edge of the quilt is curved). Cut your strips at the desired width (refer to the relevant technique for details) then join them together following one of the methods below.

JOINING STRIPS ON THE STRAIGHT

Cut the end of each strip square (at a 90-degree angle) (A). Sew the strips together end to end using ¼in seam allowance (B), then press seams open to reduce the bulk (C).

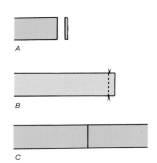

JOINING STRIPS AT A 45-DEGREE ANGLE

With this method, the seam can be less likely to show as the bulk created by the seam allowance is distributed along a larger area. Cut the end of each strip square (at a 90-degree angle) then place the ends of two strips on top of each other, right sides together, with one horizontal and the other vertical (A). Where they overlap sew at a 45-degree angle. (You can draw the sewing line on the wrong side of the fabric first if you wish.) Trim the excess fabric ¼in beyond the stitched line (B), press open and trim the ears (C).

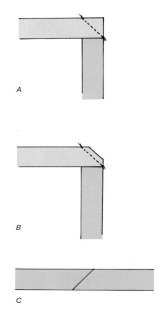

Single-Fold Binding with Straight Corners

With the single-fold binding method one layer of binding fabric is sewn and so it gives a crisp, flat finish. With straight corners, the binding is applied to two opposite sides, followed by the remaining two. Cut the strips 1¼in wide if using ¼in seam allowance and 1¾in wide if using ⅜in seam allowance.

1 Measure your quilt. Cut two strips the length of the sides plus ½in, and two strips the length of the top and bottom plus 1½in. Take the two strips for the sides and with right sides together and raw edges aligned, pin, then machine sew onto the quilt front (A).

2 Turn the quilt over so the back is facing you (B).

3 Trim the two ends of the binding strip so they are level with the sides of the quilt (C). Fold the raw edge of the binding so it is level with the edge of the quilt top. Then fold it again so it goes over the back of the quilt and covers the line from the machine sewing.

4 Sew the binding in place (D) (refer to Sewing Binding to Quilt Back).

5 Sew the top and bottom strips as before, but make sure there is an even amount of excess binding at each end.

6 Turn the quilt over so the back is facing you. Trim each end so it is about ½in longer than the quilt top. Sew as before, but before folding it down, tuck the fabric in at each end to create a hem to neaten the corners (E, F).

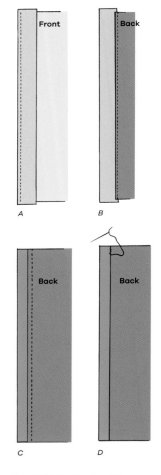

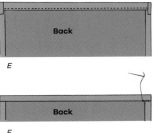

Double-Fold Binding with Mitred Corners

With the double-fold binding method the binding is folded in half before it is sewn to the quilt so it gives a firm and durable finish. Mitred corners is a folding technique that creates a neat, square finish. First decide how you are going to neaten the end of the binding as this will affect how you begin (refer to Finishing Methods 1, 2 and 3). Cut the strips 2¼in wide if using ¼in seam allowance and 2½in wide if using ⅜in seam allowance.

1 Measure the sides of your quilt. Add the four measurements together and add on 10in, then join strips to make a piece this length. Fold in half width wise, wrong sides together, and press. Aligning the raw edge of the binding with the raw edge of the front of the quilt, start sewing the binding in place, about a third of the way down one side. Try not to have the start and finish in the centre of one side as it can draw the eye towards it. Sew to the corner stopping a seam allowance width (either ¼in or ⅜in) before you get to the end (A).

2 Take the quilt from the machine and place it on a flat surface. Fold the binding up, away from the quilt, keeping the edges of the binding level with the side of the quilt (B).

3 Fold the strip back down, so that the fold is level with the edge of the quilt. Pin to hold it in place. Machine sew from the very edge of the quilt, down the side (C), once again stopping the width of the seam allowance before the end. Repeat at each corner to create a mitre.

4 Once the binding is sewn to the front of the quilt fold to the back and stitch in place (refer to Sewing Binding to Quilt Back).

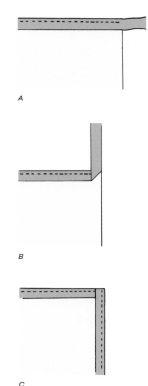

A

B

C

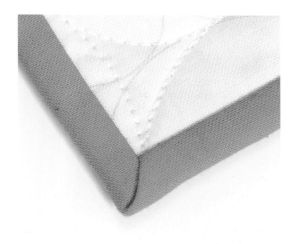

▲ *An example of double-fold binding with mitred corners.*

You can use a cup or plate as a template and cut the corners of your quilt into curves. Then cut the binding on the bias and sew it around the edge, neatly securing the start and finish using one of the finishing methods (see Finishing Methods).

SEWING BINDING TO QUILT BACK

By hand For an invisible finish, slip stitch or ladder stitch using a thread that tones with the colour of the binding. Only sew through the backing fabric and wadding (batting), not through to the front. At the corners, fold the mitre in on the back of the quilt, so it looks the same on both sides. (If you enjoy sewing embroidery stitches you could use another stitch to add a decorative finish, such as big running stitches or blanket stitch.)

By machine Either tack (baste) the binding in place or use binding clips. Slowly sew about ⅛in from the edge. You may want to make the binding slightly wider (so the back is wider than the front), so you can stitch in the ditch along the binding.

If machine sewing both sides of the binding, some people prefer to machine sew the binding to the back, then bring it round to the front after.

Finishing Methods

If you are using mitred corners, the binding will need to be neatened so that there is a secure start and finish. There are three options to choose from. The instructions are for double-fold binding, but they can be adapted for single-fold binding.

FINISHING METHOD 1

You can start the binding straight, or at a 45-degree angle, and this usually depends on the method used to join the strips together.

1 With the binding open, fold and press a ¼in hem at the beginning of the strip. Place the raw edge level with the edge of the quilt and sew about 3in (A, B).

2 Take the quilt from the machine and fold the binding so both raw edges are level with the side of the quilt. Starting about 2in away from the beginning, sew the binding (C, D), mitring the corners as you go.

3 Stop sewing about 2in from the place where you started. Trim the end of the binding so that it tucks into the gap at the beginning of the binding by about ½in. You want enough of an overlap to hide the end, but not so much that it adds bulk. Pin the join, then continue sewing to the start point (E, F).

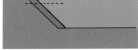

A Straight edge

B 45-degree angle

C Straight edge

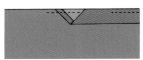

D 45-degree angle

E Straight edge

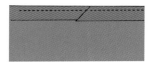

F 45-degree angle

FINISHING METHOD 2

1 Start sewing the binding leaving around a 4in length at the end unsewn. When you get to about 5in from the place where you started, take the quilt from the machine. Trim each end so that the binding overlaps by about 3in. Then fold each end of the binding back so they are flush (the folded edges should meet) and finger press (A).

2 Cut the excess fabric ¼in away from the folds, then pin and sew together, making sure the fabric is right sides together.

3 Press the seam allowance open, then pin the joined binding to the quilt. Sew over the join from the place you stopped to the start point.

A

FINISHING METHOD 3

1 Start sewing the binding leaving around a 5in length at the end unsewn. When you get to about 5in from the place where you started, take the quilt from the machine. Smooth the ends of the binding along the edge of the quilt and overlap them. Using the measurement of the width of the binding, trim the ends accordingly (for example, if the strip is 2½in wide, the overlap will be a 2½in).

2 Carefully take the quilt to the machine and join the ends of the binding with right sides together using a 45-degree seam. Lay it against the edge of the quilt to check it is the right length, then trim the excess fabric and press the seam open (A).

3 Pin the joined binding to the quilt, then sew over the join from the place you stopped to the start point.

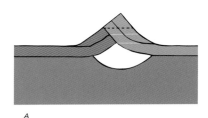

A

Not Seen Binding Techniques

These methods neaten the quilt, but the binding cannot be seen, so the design is not interrupted in any way.

BAGGED OUT METHOD

This technique is best used for smaller items such as coasters, as the backing, wadding (batting) and top must be exactly the same size or the layers may pucker. With this method, the quilting is done after the edges have been sewn, although it can also be done with a quilted panel by putting another piece of fabric on the back of it.

1 Measure the top and cut a piece of wadding and backing to exactly the same size. Place the quilt top on a table right side up, followed by the backing right side down, then the wadding. Pin to hold in place (A).

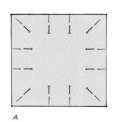

A

2 Sew around the sides, leaving a gap for turning, reverse stitching at either side of the gap so it is strong (the size of the gap will depend on the size of the item you are making but as a guide 2in is fine for a coaster and 4in for a placemat). Trim the corners (B).

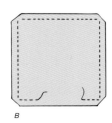

B

3 Turn the project through the gap and push out the corners. Give it a good press, folding in the hem at the gap. Sew the gap closed either by hand or on the machine (C). For a durable finish, quilt around the sides, about ¼in in from the edge.

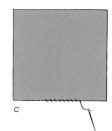

C

FACING METHOD

This method is widely used in quilts where a strong edge is needed, but the additional strip of binding seen from the front is not wanted. The width of the strip is up to personal preference but as a guide, an average width to cut is 3in, although this can be narrower for a smaller item and bigger for a larger item if you wish.

1 Measure your quilt. Cut two strips the length of the sides minus ¾in. Take the two side strips, fold them in half wrong sides together and press. Place each strip on the front of the quilt aligning the raw edges. Make sure they are centred, with an even gap at the top and bottom (about ⅜in), and sew using a ¼in seam allowance (A).

2 Fold and press the strips away from the edge of the quilt. Sew along the seam, about ⅛in away from the edge. This creates a strong edge that makes it is easier to turn (B).

3 Cut the strips for the top and bottom at least 2in longer than the width of the quilt. Place so an even amount overlaps at each end and sew. Cut the ends 1in longer than the quilt top (C).

4 Press and topstitch as before (D).

5 With the back of the quilt facing you, fold in the excess binding at the sides. Use the thickness in the sewn edge to roll it; you want a very thin line of the front of the quilt showing on the edge of the back of the quilt. Press using an iron or seam roller, then sew. Repeat with the top and bottom, but first fold the fabric in at each end of these facings to neaten the corners (E). If you find the corners are bulky, trim the excess wadding in the seam allowance at each corner.

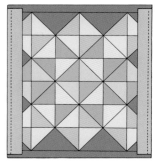

A

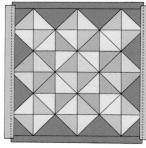

B

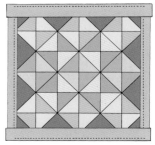

C

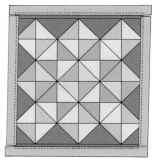

D

E

Imperial to Metric Conversions

When designing and calculating measurements for a quilt you will have a personal preference for using imperial (inches/yards) or metric (centimetres/metres) measurements. This will depend on several factors including where you live and the units used in your country, and whether you have already been taught to quilt in a specific way. The projects in this book have been written in imperial, so if you work using metric measurements you will need to convert from imperial to metric and the following advice has been provided to assist you.

To convert inches to centimetres
Multiply by 2.54
To convert yards to metres
Divide by 1.09

Here are some common quilting measurements to make your imperial to metric conversions easier.

FAT QUARTER
Measures 18 x 22in or 45.7 x 55.9cm
HALF YARD
Measures 18 x 44in or 45.7 x 111.8cm
YARD
Measures 36 x 44in or 91.4 x 111.8cm

If you work in metric, use centimetre graph paper for design and planning a project, and for cutting use rulers that have metric markings.

Smaller measurements for piecing

NOTE: THESE HAVE BEEN ROUNDED UP OR DOWN TO THE NEAREST MM

Imperial	Metric
¼in	6mm
½in	1.3cm
¾in	2cm
1in	2.5cm
1¼in	3.2cm
1½in	3.8cm
1¾in	4.4cm
2in	5.1cm
2¼in	5.7cm
2½in	6.4cm
3in	7.6cm
3½in	8.9cm
4in	10.2cm
5in	12.7cm
5½in	14cm
6½in	16.5cm
7in	17.8cm
8in	20.3cm
9in	22.9cm
9½in	24.1cm
10in	25.4cm
10½in	26.7cm
12in	30.5cm
12½in	31.8cm
18in	45.7cm

Larger measurements for purchasing fabric

NOTE: THESE HAVE BEEN ROUNDED UP TO THE NEAREST 5CM

Imperial	Metric
¼yd	0.25m
⅜yd	0.35m
½yd	0.50m
⅝yd	0.60m
¾yd	0.70m
⅞yd	0.80m
1yd	0.95m
1⅛yd	1.05m
1¼yd	1.15m
1⅜yd	1.30m
1½yd	1.40m
1⅝yd	1.50m
1¾yd	1.65m
1⅞yd	1.75m
2yd	1.85m
2⅛yd	1.95m
2¼yd	2.10m
2⅜yd	2.20m
2½yd	2.30m
2⅝yd	2.45m
2¾yd	2.55m
3yd	2.75m
3¼yd	3m
3½yd	3.25m
4yd	3.70m

Templates

These templates are all shown at actual size.

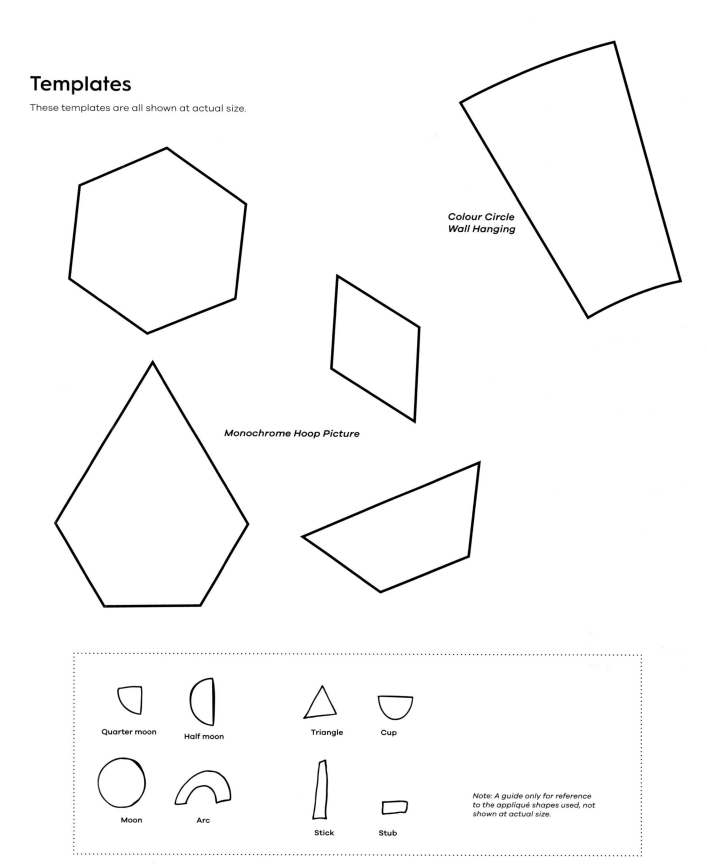

*Colour Circle
Wall Hanging*

Monochrome Hoop Picture

Quarter moon

Half moon

Triangle

Cup

Moon

Arc

Stick

Stub

*Note: A guide only for reference
to the appliqué shapes used, not
shown at actual size.*

Acknowledgements

Thank you to the David and Charles team, particularly Sarah and Jeni for offering me this opportunity and making everything look wonderful. A special mention to my editor – thank you Cheryl for your support, critique and help in bringing all the strands in this book together.

Closer to home, much thanks and love to my family, Darren, Jude and Florence, for never batting an eyelid at various sewing-related items being strewn around our home and never complaining when a work colleague or school-friend points out that, yet again, you have thread hanging off you. Also, to my mum who has helped out with things such as giving teenagers lifts so I can work extra hours, as well as being lovely quilt company when coming along to various talks and events over the years.

To my hugely talented textiles network, Sara Cook, Wendy Ward, Suzanne Fisher, Carolyn Clark, Amanda Want, Nicole Lichtenberg and Leslie Morgan. My gratitude goes out to you for not just being lovely people, but for your knowledge, work and encouragement that is always an inspiration to my textiles journey and my life.

Finally, to my students, past and present: it is a joy to sew along with others, and to feel your enthusiasm when I am sharing my skills with you always puts a spring in my step. All the years demonstrating and explaining quilt design and construction have made me a better craftsperson by far. Often teaching classes does not feel like work, but just spending time doing what I love with friendly people, and for that I am very grateful.

Contributors

The author would like to pay tribute to the talented designers whose work appears in this book.

Karen Ackva
www.easypatchwork.de

Janae Bissinger

Katie Clark Blakesley
www.swimbikequilt.com

Susan Briscoe
www.susanbriscoe.com

Julia Davis & Anne Muxworthy

Brigit Dermott
www.brigitgail.com

Malka Dubrawsky
www.stitchindye.com

Tanya Finken

Brioni Greenberg
www.instagram.com/flossyblossy

Debbie Grifka
www.debbiegrifka.com

Caroline Hadley
www.geometriquilt.com

Juliet van der Hejden
www.thetartankiwi.com

Kacia Hosmer
www.coconutrobot.com

Kevin Kosbab
www.feeddog.net

Penny Layman
www.sewtakeahike.typepad.com

Karen Lewis
www.karenlewistextiles.com

Pam & Nicky Lintott
www.quiltroom.co.uk

Sandy Maxfield
www.sandystardesigns.com

Sarah J Maxwell
www.designsbysarahj.com

Coleen Merte
www.northwaterquilts.com

Angela Pingel
www.angelapingel.com

Catherine Redford
www.catherineredford.com

Rebecca Severt
www.creativeblockquilts.blogspot.com

Zeena Shah
www.zeenashah.com

Lucie Summers
www.etsy.com/shop/summersville

Gina Tell
www.thread-graffiti.com

Suppliers

Brighton Sewing Centre
68 North Road
Brighton
BN1 1YD
www.brightonsewingcentre.co.uk

Eclectic Maker
Station Parade
3 Tarring Road
Worthing
BN11 4SS
www.eclecticmaker.co.uk

Raystitch
66-68 Essex Road
London
N1 8LR
raystitch.co.uk

Sew Hot
3b Holly Road
Thornton-Cleveleys
FY5 4HH
www.sewhot.co.uk

Olive + Flo Handcraft
oliveandflohandcraft.co.uk

M is for Make
www.misformake.co.uk

Bloomerie Fabrics
www.bloomeriefabrics.com

The Natural Loom
www.thenaturalloom.com.au

Useful Links

The Modern Quilt Guild
Founded in the USA by Alissa Haight Carlton and Latifah Saafir in 2009. They have local groups, offer individual membership and organise Quilt Con, the world's largest quilt show dedicated to modern quilting.

www.themodernquiltguild.com/modern-quilting

The Modern Quilt Group
Based in the UK, this is a specialist subgroup of The Quilters' Guild of the British Isles.

modern-quilt.quiltersguild.org.uk

About the Author

PHOTO CREDIT: Emma Kennedy

Elizabeth Betts is a Brighton-based quilt designer and textile artist. After attending London College of Fashion and the University of East London she accidentally fell in love with quilting in the early 2000s while looking for a small project to fill in the last day of a dressmaking summer school. Two years of sampler classes with Sara Cook in Hove were followed by her studying for a City and Guilds in Patchwork and Quilting with the art quilter Janet Twinn in Surrey.

A keen writer and quilt history enthusiast, she wrote a paper titled The Role of Liberty in the post 1960s UK Quilt Revival, which was published by the British Quilt Study Group in 2010. This was followed by her first book, The Beginner's Guide to Quilting, published by F&W in 2013, which led in turn to her to presenting quilt tutorials on Quilt Daily.

A popular tutor, in 2010 Elizabeth opened Quilty Pleasures, a modern quilting shop/studio from where she ran regular workshops and hosted guest tutors. The studio closed in 2015, so she could concentrate more on project work, which has included editing Popular Patchwork magazine, acting as a mentor in the textile art sector, and working as a facilitator for the 2018 Jane Austen's House Museum community quilt project, which was funded by the Heritage Lottery Fund.

Elizabeth lives in Brighton, a vibrant seaside city where eccentric Regency design juxtaposes with 1960s architecture, which provides her with more ideas than she has time to turn into reality. Her latest project has seen her combine narratives from local history with design based on architecture to create abstract quilts to teach in a local community setting.

Index

The publisher and author would like to thank all of the talented designers and photographers whose work features in this book.

A DAVID AND CHARLES BOOK
© David and Charles, Ltd 2019

David and Charles is an imprint of David and Charles, Ltd
1 Emperor Way, Exeter Business Park, Exeter, EX1 3QS

Text and Projects © Elizabeth Betts, Ltd 2019
Layout and Photography © David and Charles, Ltd 2019,
except pages 34, 46, 79 and 84 © Joe Hancock

First published in the UK and USA in 2019

A catalogue record for this book is available from the British Library.

ISBN-13: 9781446307465 paperback
ISBN-13: 9781446378717 EPUB

Printed in China by Hong Kong Graphics for:
David and Charles, Ltd
1 Emperor Way, Exeter Business Park, Exeter, EX1 3QS

10 9 8 7 6 5 4 3 2 1

Content Director: Ame Verso
Senior Commissioning Editor: Sarah Callard
Managing Editor: Jeni Hennah
Project Editor: Cheryl Brown
Design Manager: Anna Wade
Design and Art Direction: Sarah Rowntree
Illustrations: Sarah Rowntree and Emma Teagle
Photographer: Jason Jenkins
Production Manager: Beverley Richardson

David and Charles publishes high quality books on a wide range of subjects.
For more information visit www.davidandcharles.com.

Layout of the digital edition of this book may vary depending on reader hardware and display settings.